CW00666552

THE GIRL BEHIND THE WALL

By Antje Arnold

I want to thank my mom for not only traveling back in time with me, but also for allowing me to relive my childhood memories with her.

Also, a big Thank you goes out to my husband and kids who inspired me to write this story.

Index

Foreword:

I decided to write this book not merely as a memory archive for myself, but also as a "personal history" piece for my children. It's meant as a "walk back in time" to a world that no longer exists and can no longer be touched or felt. I know there is the "DDR Museum" in Berlin, Germany that provides you with a great overview of the world gone by. I highly recommend it to anyone who wants to learn more about East Germany. Sometimes, however, it's those private stories of personal experiences that create a better view of the world I grew up in.

My family is rather small and does not extend far beyond my parents. Both of them grew up in an orphanage, each for different reasons and under different circumstances. Therefore, I did not have the opportunity or privilege of growing up listening to stories told by my grandparents, aunts, and uncles, about the past. I met my paternal grandfather and my maternal grandmother only a couple of times, and neither one of them talked to me about my parents or what the world was like in their own times. It's rather sad, and if I had the chance to meet them again, I would probably ask more specific questions, but the time is gone and cannot be reclaimed.

One day I woke up and decided to make it my mission to retell my story, as simplistic as it might be. This will be part of the legacy I leave for my kids because there won't be anyone else left who can tell it.

This book and the story within is not meant to glorify the ways of East German living, nor to excuse anything that happened. It's written from my personal viewpoint as a child; without the struggles of adult life and their views of their world at that time. The book is not intended to deliver any specific historic insight or provide accurate data you would see in a documentary. I'm not going to describe the world from an adult's point of view, because I can assure you that it will not match mine; at least not from that time period. This book is also not supposed to be a sappy story, but merely a throwback in time – a different perspective from what most "westerners" think East Germany was like. I will bet that when it comes to being a child in that world, they are all wrong.

Go ahead and read for yourself, though.

The Girl Behind the German Wall

This is the story of a girl growing up behind the German wall. Keep in mind, however, you were also behind the wall, just on the other side. Maybe all the stories you were told about us are not actually true. Many people have this misconception that growing up behind the "iron curtain" must have been a terrible thing. I will let you be the judge of that....

To be quite honest, it was not bad at all – for me, at least. I didn't miss out on anything because I didn't know what I was missing. Just like any small child, I didn't look far beyond my front yard or apartment building or wherever else I was roaming around. As a child, nothing matters more than what is directly going on around you. I wouldn't trade my childhood with anybody in the world. It was unforgettable, memorable, and, in hindsight, historical. Looking back on it as an adult, I now realize that it was so much more than that. Where you come from or grow up shapes you as a person. It provides you with roots and a feeling of belonging; a place you will always call home and never leave; at least in your heart. East Germany makes me appreciate the things I have in my life today more than anybody could imagine. I can tell stories that remind most people of tales from their grandparents - only, in this case, it happened to me and all my friends in the 80s. My life is part of world history and I am eminently proud of that.

I was born a second child, a little sister for my brother. Overall, I had to go through the same troubles as any other younger siblings; fighting, arguing, disagreeing, and some occasional fun times.

Both of my parents worked full-time, as did the majority of adults. I can point out only one person who was a stay-at-home mom due to a disability. Other than that, it was all but unheard of for a parent to stay home – unless they were on maternity leave, of course.

During the first few years of my life I grew up in a town about thirty kilometers east of Berlin and also about thirty kilometers west of the Polish border. We lived in a one-bedroom apartment, but moved to the suburban area when I was about to enter second grade in 1986. In the apartment, I shared the one available bedroom with my brother. My parents did their best to divide it with a wall of furniture to give us some sort of privacy, but that only worked half of the time. As you can imagine, sibling rivalry and the claiming of space and property were in full force during daytime hours. However, during the night we called a truce. I slept next to the only window and spent most of my nights looking outside and searching for patterns in the stairway lights of the apartment building across from me. I know that sounds weird, but I was about five years old and looking for patterns in every aspect of my life. Sleeping was never one of my favorite things. It was like my body rebelled against it, or at least I felt that it did. I have no idea where my energy for the day ahead came from, because after staying up most of the nights I had to still get up very early in the morning. For some reason, I found looking out the window fascinating. It's not like there was much going on outside, but I just loved observing everything.

My parents slept in the living room on an orange-brown fold-out couch. They had to make their bed every morning and turn it back into a couch for the day. They stuffed their pillows, sheet, and blankets into the wall cabinets, which incidentally were also a great place for "hide-and-seek".

The kitchen was small; no more than a galley kitchen, really. There was a small table to sit at by the window, very cozy, and yet practical. It was a very white kitchen; white tiles, white oven and white cabinets. The large window let in a lot of light and made the room feel bigger than it really was. You would also find my little brown wooden stepping stool in there. Well, you found it everywhere I was. As a small child with a big adventurous heart and immense curiosity, I wanted to be able to gain access whenever and wherever I was. I have no idea where this little stool came from or who gave it to me. I do not even know if it was truly mine. I did claim it, though. It was almost an extension of myself, and there are pictures to prove it. I would use it as my chair to "read" my Russian magazines, a ladder to reach for my drink on the counter or climb up onto it to sneak candy, as a bed for any of my stuffed animals, as higher ground from which to observe my mom's cooking or anything else I could think of. It was my very own multi-tool.

You would not find a microwave, dishwasher or huge refrigerator in any kitchen. Americans would classify our refrigerator as a dorm fridge. I found it quite convenient, because it was the perfect height for me, whether I was helping to set the table or handing over any baking ingredients to my mom.

The bathroom was on the smaller size as well, but it also had a big window on the end. We had a bathtub, of course, but I guess the sink worked just fine for a quick wash down. There was some overhead storage right above the door for items such as the laundry basket, detergent, cleaners, towels clothes pins and soaps. Did I mention it had cactus green walls? It was quite ugly. I have no clue who decided on the paint, but even as a kid I found the color choice very odd. However, my dad would turn the bathroom into his occasional photography lab; maybe green was a great light dimmer.

My mom had one of those huge, awkward washing machines in the bathroom, but she had to go down to the basement of the apartment building to dry the clothes. There was a signup sheet on the first floor by the apartment entrance where you picked the date on which you were going to hang up your clothes. This assured the right number of people had a time slot without running out of clothes-line space. It was always a steam bath down there. You couldn't see a thing when everyone was barricading the view with their wet laundry. It created a slight cloud of fog due to the high room temperature. My favorite part was when they hung towels and bedsheets because it created perfect obstacles you could run around and hide behind. As you can imagine, nobody appreciated our playtime in the "drying room" and we were chased out a million times.

Apartment living was fun, most of the time. Everyone liked me, but they were always worried because I was usually hollering about something. I was not a spoiled brat by any means. I just got myself into certain situations which I insisted I could take care of myself. I guess you could say I had a reputation for proving my independence at every opportunity. This usually started by convincing everybody to let me be and stating that I didn't need any help, and then about five minutes later they would hear me scream. I might have fallen down the steps, or tripped going up, with something in my hands, or any other possible thing you can imagine. But people liked me in spite of that, because I was cute, kind and well-behaved. I was never a whiny kid. If anything, I was an adventurer at heart and usually on some type of "important" mission. I had a huge imagination and always found something to do. We had a neighbor on the upper floor who would throw toys out of his window all the time. Sometimes, he would even throw our toys out the window when he came to visit with his parents. As you can imagine, my parents, especially my dad, did not appreciate this type of behavior at all. Unfortunately, it was my brother who received the blame for it. I cannot say for certain, but I believe that kid was not invited to our flat anymore after that scenario. Toys were not something we received very often. That's why we took care of them to our best abilities.

I always thought my brother had the better toys. Even though my own craft collection was something to be jealous of, I usually found myself playing with his toys. Sometimes I played with his action figures by lining them up in a half-circle and then threw them down with a plastic cap from a squeezable plastic bottle.

Other times, I created entire farms with his toy animals, fences and barns. I'm not sure if he cared or just never found out I was playing with them, but I definitely had a marvelous time entertaining myself.

One time my mom bought a tiny toy truck for us. The truck was about the size of a matchbox car, but made entirely out of plastic. It was light blue with a red steering wheel, black tires and a light yellow housing. You could open the driver and passenger doors, as well as the double door at the end. It was great, because it seemed so realistic. I loved cars, even as a girl. One day, I decided to take my truck outside to play. Along the side of the apartment building, you could always find a trail of ants in the summer time; tons of them. I would step on them, squash them or interfere with their trail in some sort of way. I know what you are thinking, but just remember all your ant traps in your own house right now.

On that particular day, I lost my truck and was convinced that those ants not only took it from me, but also drove away with it. I know it sounds absurd, but I was about 4 years old and in my mind, I had a case that called for an investigation. My parents didn't quite believe me, but I was certain about it and checked many times to see if my little truck showed up again. Plus, I just liked giving those ants my evil eye for stealing it in the first place. Needless to say, I never saw it again.

All the kids in the neighborhood played outside, regardless of the weather; unless it was raining. There was a huge sandcastle the size of a backyard swimming pool. We would build tunnels and play with our cars, and our cowboys, and Indians action figures. Those were the only action figures we had, but they were perfect. Yes, we were raised with the whole Good vs Evil thing - based on the movie adventures of "Old Shatterhand and Winnetou". They were blood brothers and got along just fine.

You did not find any fancy swing sets or slides, but some sort of mushroom monkey bar thing. The main goal was to get on top of the round roof. I was, as usual, too short, and could never get my legs around the poles to push myself onto the roof top. I had a daily goal and was committed.

The wonderful thing about the neighborhood was that you didn't have to worry about cars because only a few people actually owned one. Most people got their driver's license at the legal age of eighteen, but then were put on a waiting list to receive the actual car. My dad waited sixteen years to get his Trabant. It was green and my mom hated the color.

I know the description of the playground doesn't sound super exciting, but believe me, -- our imaginations were endless. We regularly made up some kind of game that would occupy us for hours at a time. We also had a great sledding hill a bit farther away. There were horses there in the spring and summer, but when winter arrived it turned into a giant sledding area. We would go down that hill at probably ten miles an hour! It was warp speed in our eyes. You just had to watch out for the pond and the big tree at the bottom of the hill. The tree stood in the middle of the frozen pond. We had to steer carefully or else we would plow right into it. I really didn't like winter very much when I was younger, because I would get cold very quickly. The only way I was able to stay out in the cold at all, was to keep myself busy building snowmen, snow forts and sledding. Once my feet got cold, the fun times were over and I walked home to thaw my toes and fingers.

Summer was my favorite season. My mom didn't appreciate some of my outdoor adventures, though. In particular, she despised the times when I would race all the way to the third floor; ring the doorbell and present her with a "sick" bird. Instead of rushing me inside to take care of the poor little creature, she would simply slam the door in my face and leave me totally devastated. It wasn't her fault - apparently the bird was dead. I thought it was sick, and my mom was supposed to come to the rescue and make it all better. It turned out she was not that kind of miracle worker. Still, having your mom slam the doors in your face isn't reassuring. She spared me the angry lecture and just made it clear that no dead animals were allowed inside.

Looking back, I feel bad, that I questioned everything. Why is the bird dead?", "Why can I not eat those orange berries on the tree?", "Why do we walk everywhere?", "Why does this guy look funny?", "Why does he have blue scribbles on his arm?", "Why can I not drink vinegar?" I must have been in my "Why" phase for a long time. I also didn't take people at face value just because they knew my parents. Never. I was extremely suspicious of people in general and preferred to observe them from a distance first. People always labeled me as "shy", when in all reality I was observing people to figure out what they were all about and whether I considered them to be "good, trustworthy people". I believe my dad tested my suspicious nature more than anyone. He liked to tell stories about daily things, people and events. I did not take those stories as truth either. Maybe I should have, because it was my dad after all, but I didn't and kept digging deeper by asking more questions when his stories seemed not to be 'logical'- it always had to be 'logical' to me and, therefore, plausible and true. So, fibbing usually did not work at all, - but that didn't stop them from trying.

We also had a dog, usually a dachshund, because my dad was a hunter and he bred dachshunds. I liked our dog, but when she was pregnant and had puppies, she turned into a mama bear and scared me with her growls. I know, it's natural, but her bed was in the only bathroom and using it became a harrowing experience. I used to avoid eye contact and pretended she wasn't there in hopes she'd do the same for me. It only worked occasionally, and I had to announce my bathroom trips to my parents just to make them aware of any possible "trauma."

As you can imagine, apartment living, could be a bit boring. On rainy days it was the worst, because I was stuck inside and had to entertain myself in a small room that I shared with my older brother. I generally found something to do, but I had to make sure my activities were not interfering with my brother's space. My favorite indoor pastimes were puzzles, and not just any puzzles. My puzzles were pictures of castles, lakes and forests with a minimum of one thousand pieces. I don't know how my interest in puzzles began, but I loved them and had quite a collection of them. Also, I liked arts and crafts. Anything to keep my hands and mind busy, because I couldn't sit still and would get 'antsy' when I had nothing to do. I was always on a mission to complete some sort of project.

Another hobby of mine was tending to my vast stamp collection. I guess my sense of adventure and travel started early in my childhood. Since we couldn't travel outside the country, I made it my mission to collect as many unique stamps as possible. This all started with me cutting out the stamps of any letters or postcards we received. As soon as I had a handful of stamps collected, I would submerge them in the bathroom sink filled with warm water. Once the stamps were all soaked properly, I loosened them and separated the stamps from the paper. Then it was all about the drying process, which meant keeping them flat without having them stick to the paper again or turning into ugly, crinkly, tiny pictures. I was not an expert by any means, but was figuring this all out on my own. Thankfully my parents were very supportive and even collected stamps from other people who had received letters and cards.

I had a thick blue stamp album and carefully inserted all my stamps. We had a paper store in town that also carried stamps and I loved going there. I honestly didn't have a particular preference in the type of stamps I collected, but they had to look appealing to me in some sort of way. When I was about five or six years old, I loved anything colorful, especially when the stamps came in a set of six to ten and told some sort of story. That's when I started collecting comic book stamps. Little did I know back then, but I was collecting Disney stamps? Obviously, I had no idea who these characters were, but I just liked all the Mickey Mouse, Donald Duck, Pinocchio, 101 Dalmatians, etc. stamps. I loved all my stamps and rearranged them often. I liked simply looking at them and taking in every detail. As with any collection, I had my favorite. One stamp I loved in particular was a 3D stamp. I didn't care about the fact that it was some sort of ice hockey scene, but just loved the 3D effect of it. In case you are wondering; yes, I still have it to this day.

Sometimes, when you bought a stamp collection set, you were also given a special envelope along with it. I always loved the gold embellishments on them. It made them extra special to me. At some point, my brother decided to start his own collection of stamps and it became a bit of a competition between the two of us. Who could get to the mail first and cut the stamp off the letter? I don't think he was as dedicated as me, but he did have some cool stamps. On the whole, collecting stamps was really my own way of connecting with the world, with places that I was not able to visit or explore on my own. It's funny, because I really cared only about the stamps, not so much about what people were writing in their letters or on their postcards.

I also had a slight obsession with organizing things. You might call it OCD. At a young age, I would already organize everything by size. All the books were aligned from tall to short and from wide to narrow. My little knickknacks were arranged in perfectly straight or angled lines, as well as by size, color, themes and favorites. After organizing my books, clothes, school supplies and collectibles, I would eventually move on to my brother's side of the room. He did not always appreciate me messing with his "stuff," but gave me a pass in the end since it meant he didn't have to do it.

My mom is very talented at knitting, crocheting, and sewing. One day, I asked her if I could try to knit as well. She gladly provided me with blue yarn and knitting needles and showed me patiently how to use them to make a scarf. I thought it would be easy because she would always knit away and not even look at her hands! I did pretty well after completing my first few rows and decided I would continue in my room. I sat on the floor and focused on the task at hand. It was an absolute disaster. I became so frustrated with myself and, of course, blamed it on the blue yarn. It could not possibly be my fault. I threw the yarn and needles in front of me on the floor and gave it a piece of my mind, then decided that it was still too close for comfort and kicked it further away. Eventually, I stood up, picked up the yarn, and threw it across the room! That made me feel much better. In the end, I did pick it up from behind my brother's dresser and gave it back to my mom, admitting that this "mindless" craft was just not my style. I have not picked up knitting again since then and I am quite happy to leave this hobby to the experts.

I preferred playing outside. There was plenty of space, and it was the perfect setting to let my imaginations run wild. Our apartment buildings were set up in rows close together, so we always had plenty of friends to play with. Our parents never really had to worry about some stranger coming by and doing something rotten to us kids. Overall, it was a safe environment to grow up in.

My dad was absent a lot during the week when we lived in the apartment. He was going to school to be a police officer. I often slept next to my mom on the foldout couch. My favorite part about that was her reading me a bedtime story every night. She usually let me pick between the "Brothers Grimm Tales" and "The Struwwelpeter". I loved books! I couldn't wait to read on my own.

My mom had a special connection with the owner of the bookstore in town. Apparently, her daughter went to the Kindergarten where my mom worked. Due to this connection, my mom was able to order books for me that most people did not have access to. I still have my first "special" book my mom bought from her and it was always my favorite. It was a book about a Panda and an Asian family. I loved the simple story and the drawings inside. The story and characters were total opposites of my life and I'm sure that was a big part of why I was so drawn to it. A few other books were Fantasy story books about adventures of trolls and wizards. I still have all those books from that time and would not ever want to part with them.

When we moved to our house in the country a few years later, I became best friends with the librarian. Our library was in the center of town, across the train tracks. For some reason, I always decided to ride my bike to the library when the train was rolling in. I guess it never occurred to me to check the train schedule. I enjoyed reading so much that I showed up at the library at least two to three times a week and usually borrowed between five to ten books each time. The library itself was not very big at all, maybe the size of a living room or small classroom. The bookshelves were arranged in all sorts of directions to make the most of the small space and even touched the ceiling. The desk of the white-haired librarian was all the way in the back of the room, but you could always see her as soon as you entered. My library card was covered in time stamps; front and back. It didn't take long to collect those date stamps and I had to get a new card. I never truly cared about any specific genres then, but initially picked the books based on the title and cover picture. I would borrow anything from fiction to non-fiction, practical books like building birdhouses, gardening and cooking. However, I did enjoy fantasy books the most, because they were all about adventures and places I so badly wanted to visit one day. On rare occasions, I ran out of ideas what to read about and usually ended up chatting with the librarian about her suggestions for me. Reading is still a big part of my life today and always will be.

My great-grandmother's house

As mentioned earlier, my father grew up in an orphanage. His dad left at some point in his early life for reasons unknown to me, and his mom passed away in a train accident when he was very young. His grandmother was the only person who still gave him a sense of family, and even though he was in the orphanage, he was able to go to her house during the holidays.

My dad's grandmother had a small white house with a red terracotta shingled roof and a big yard in the country. It was located about 6 km from where we lived in the suburbs. The house had two stories, but the attic was not useable at all. You could go up there and walk around, but it was not really suitable as a living space. I guess you could have used it for storage of some sort because adults could not really stand up in it and you could only get to it with a ladder from the outside. When you walked into the house, you straight away entered the room that was used as a kitchen. It was extremely narrow and no more than one person could be in that space at the same time. Even as a small child I found it claustrophobic. If you stood in front of the cabinet, you only had to take a single step back to touch the wall. The kitchen had everything aligned on the right side of the wall; a big white cupboard for dishes, glasses, cups and a sink. It was the most basic, bare-bones kitchen arrangement I had ever seen. She did have running water in the kitchen, but only cold water was available. There was no refrigerator. There was a door on the floor which provided access to a small cellar where she stored vegetables, jars of jelly and smoked sausages. This was considered her "cold room" and used for all other perishable items, such as milk, butter and fresh meat. Since most people only purchased food items for a couple days at a time, you did not have to worry about your groceries spoiling.

From the kitchen, you entered directly into the big common room. It was her room for everything. On the left side stood a single bed (next to a tall tile oven), and on the right side was a tall dresser, next to the vanity-like table where her TV sat. There was one big window in the room which had her table and two chairs in front of it. She also had one big "sitting" chair in the middle of the room. I think it was positioned that way so she could look outside. She lived by herself, because her husband had passed away in WWII. We usually visited her every Saturday and Sunday during the warm weather. My mom would cook a hot lunch at the apartment and then pack everything up to take to my great-grandma's house because we would spend the entire day there. The packing always included drinks, cups, utensils, plates, etc. I assume because there was not enough at the house for all of us to use.

We rode our bikes to her house every single time, and due to the lack of space, we never stayed overnight. My brother had his own bike; it was a silver and Bordeaux color. I would usually sit on a tiny leather seat in the front of either my mom's or my dad's bicycle. I always wanted to ride on my own, but I was too small and too short for a bike. I often felt guilty about adding extra weight to the load, because my mom already had so much "stuff" to carry, so I tried my best to sit perfectly still to not throw her off balance. The ride on the main road was usually very peaceful due to the lack of cars and trucks. The roads were lined with big trees on both sides and provided plenty of shade with just the right amount of sunlight to not feel blocked off from the world around us. There were a few sections that cut straight through the woods and small garden communities. My favorite part was the ability to merely observe and inspect my surroundings as the road led us on to our destination. It never got old despite the fact that we took the exact same path every time. There seemed to be an ever-changing environment; new birds, rabbits, squirrels, bushes, and fruit trees. I truly enjoyed being engrossed in it all, finding peace in the consistency and simplicity of my life.

I don't recall ever spending a rainy day at my great grandmother's house, most likely because we stayed home during inclement weather. The bathroom situation was not very pleasant at her house. From the description above, you may have noticed that I didn't mention a bathroom.

She didn't actually have one. She had an outhouse directly attached to the main building. I tried to avoid it as much as possible. Honestly, I preferred to do my business in the woods. I hated the outhouse that much. In my defense, it was dark! As soon as you closed the dark wooden door, there was no light coming in besides the little sunbeams penetrating through the door lock and around the frame. I truly cannot emphasize enough how thankful I was that we usually left before it turned dark outside. It smelled bad and the seat was basically a round wooden hole with a lid. Considering my size, that particular opening might as well have been a crater. I was petrified of falling into it. It was a true nightmare. Don't judge me for my decision to prefer Mother Nature's bathroom. It was a lot safer!

On the upside, her garden and overall property was huge! At least it seemed that way to someone my size – I would estimate that it was probably nearly two acres. My favorite part were all the fruit trees in her yard. I believe she had at least 5 different apple trees, a pear tree, a plum tree, and a sour cherry tree. My dad had his garden there as well and always planted strawberries, lettuce, radishes, carrots and snap peas.

Also, there were two big sheds next to the house. One was for garden tools and general yard equipment, and the other was for my dad's birds and bees. No, really – birds and bees. My dad had wild pheasants, gold pheasants, Zebra Finches, some type of wild chicken, Love Birds and budgies. I certainly enjoyed them a lot, because they were pretty and were interesting to watch, but the honey bees were an entirely different story.

He had about fifteen bee hives. Now, you might think "how cool" and "you could make your own honey."

That was certainly true, and I always enjoyed the entire process of spinning the honey; it was a manual job, which meant sore arms at the end of the day. As with any homemade food, the honey tasted delicious and was more flavorful than anything you could have bought in the store. Trust me; there is absolutely nothing better than a fresh buttered roll with your very own, hand-spun honey.

However, there was one major downside to this entire project: the bees did not like me. At least, that was my assumption at the early age of five. Why? Every day of the weekend I got stung! Not just one sting, but usually an average of five at the same time- on top of my head. I was not a happy camper. I would run to whoever was closest and had them swat the bees. I can't remember if I suffered any headaches because of that, but I certainly remember the pain from the bee stings. I tried to avoid the beehive area as much as possible, but then my dad would ask me to help him, and while he was all covered in his protective gear, all I got was a glove to hold something for him. I did like the little smoke pump we used to make the bees drowsy, though. I might have gone overboard with it a few times, but I loved the mere mechanism of it and for some reason, I liked the scent of it. Apparently, I was a lot braver than my older brother. He would just run like a maniac when bees were close to him, let alone stinging him. That made me feel a little bit better. My dad was very impressed by how I never freaked out and just handled the situation in the calmest way possible. I guess, that after being stung a "million" times, I knew what to expect.

I really enjoyed being at my great-grandmother's house, even though I don't think she actually cared for me that much. Maybe it was because of the time I decided to climb up into the attic and drop rocks down the small opening of a chimney-looking thing. I just liked the noise it made when I was dropping the rocks. I didn't know that the rocks landed in her "kitchen." I stopped after my dad scolded me, but I think she bore a grudge towards me ever since. Fortunately, the yard was big enough to keep me busy all day and every day, so I could avoid her presence as much as possible. If I seemed to have disappeared, I was most likely sitting in one of the apple trees. I loved apples. It seems I was eating an apple every very single picture ever taken of me. It's a bit weird, I know, but at least I have proof.

Her house was the last one on the street, which gave way to dirt roads, cornfields, and forest. My brother and I would play in the cornfields all the time. One day we decided that each of us would take a long stick and create "rooms" in the field for us. We made a big circle in the field for designated "rooms"; the living room, the kitchen, the bathroom and the hallway. Pushing down those big, tall stalks of corn was a lot of work and took us almost the entire afternoon. Basically, we created crop circles; only we didn't know that term back then. We played "house" and had a blast. We never considered the consequences; after all, we were just kids ages five and eight. As you can imagine, the crop circles didn't leave the same positive impression on the person who actually owned the field. He had a conversation with my dad, and dad made certain to relay the message to us. The man was extremely unhappy about our exploits and made us put the cornstalks right again. That was even more work than knocking them down. I still wonder, though, what our circles looked like from above. It certainly would have been interesting.

That was the last time we flattened any crops, so we decided to venture into the forest behind the cornfield. It was thick with tall trees, some fallen and little openings where the sun would beam through extra bright. We also found a small water hole. It seemed so out of place, almost weird.

One day we took our fishing rods to the water hole to find out if anything was living in it.

Surprisingly, we did catch a couple fish and declared it our very own personal fishing spot. The best part was that nobody else knew about it. After bringing back our fish, my dad became curious; probably wondering what trouble we caused this time. However, he decided to go with us and was as amazed what we discovered. He decided to join us on our next fishing trip and brought a net. We caught about eight fish and took them back to my great-grandmother's house and put them in a small metal tub outside in the yard. That way the fish could swim around before we would prepare them for dinner. As it turned out, it was quite fortunate that we had that particular tub in the yard that day.

I was eating cherries under the tree in my bare feet, (as usual), and stepped on a wasp. As you can imagine, it stung like crazy. The first thing I saw was the metal tub. I hopped towards it and stuck my injured foot into the cold water to bring the swelling down and to alleviate my discomfort. I can still remember how good the water felt and how weird it was to have the fish swimming around my foot. It didn't take long for my dad to catch me with my foot in the water, so my cooling techniques was short-lived. I hobbled to the bench and sat down and analyze the "damage." The bottom of my foot was quite swollen, but it certainly wasn't unpleasant enough to convince me to wear shoes. Being in my bare feet was liberating, and I took advantage of it as much as possible. I only put sandals on when it was time to go home. On other occasions, my brother and I would go "exploring." We would just walk around the dirt roads and alongside other houses further down the street. People generously decorated their front yards by planting all sorts of different flowers and rose bushes. Sometimes we would pick the flowers sticking through the fences and create a nice bouquet for my mom. She loved them, at least until she found out where they had come from. Of course, we felt guilty at the time, but we really did have good intentions and it was always meant as a nice gesture in appreciation for everything my mom did for us. No worries, we did not repeat this sort of flower larceny.

One time, while "exploring" our surrounding area, we found a building site. It was still in the very early stages of a future residence. Basically, it was a big hole in the ground – with lots of building sand. It looked like a great sandbox. No, really, how were we supposed to stay away? Curiosity got the best of us and off we went - into the big sandbox. We found tons of toads, both adults and babies! I was very excited and thought they were adorable. There was no way I could possibly leave them behind in the hot sand. I decided to find them a better and more suitable home, but first I wanted my mom to see them. I carried about five tiny hopping baby toads in my hands to surprise her. She did not share my excitement and did not enjoy the up-close and personal display of baby toads. She insisted that I let them go free before they peed on my hands and gave me warts. Remember, I was never a gullible child and continually questioned everything! My observation told me that they had not peed on my hand at that point, so I decided to keep them around a bit longer. I was also not concerned with getting any warts – since they didn't mess in my hand, how could I possibly get them? My logic certainly made sense me. My mom just rolled her eyes and left. I guess, she always knew which battles were worth fighting. Off I went with my toads. Don't worry; I was never mean to any animals, and I took them into the forest near the water hole. I thought they would be happier there than inside the sandbox. Of course, my parents also reminded us to not walk on others' property – ever. Trust me, if my dad said it, you were always better off going along with his point of view. He was my hero in many ways, and growing up I wanted to be just like him, but you definitely did not want to be on his angry side.

Daycare aka Kindergarten

First of all, let me tell you that Kindergarten was an entirely separate entity from school. Preschool and Kindergarten were not in any way connected to an actual school building, but a separate facility altogether.

I went to daycare where my mom worked. As a matter of fact, that was the only reason I was able to go to Kindergarten to begin with. Apparently, my pediatrician advised against exposing me to crowds of kids, because I got sick so often. However, because my mom worked right next door at the preschool, my doctor gave me a pass and let me join the crowd. My Kindergarten was close to our apartment and occasionally I would walk home by myself. Yes, we are talking about crossing a major road. Looking back, I realize my parents must have really trusted me with my road safety skills. Then again, in their defense, -there were not very many cars.

I loved preschool and Kindergarten. It was an all-day event and I had to get up at 5 a.m. to get ready. We habitually listened to the same radio show in the morning. It was kind of a reality show in its own way and gave you an inside look at a family with three kids. They essentially had the same issues as any regular family. There were stories of smelly hidden sandwiches from lunches long ago, forgotten homework, fighting amongst the children or just running late in general. When the radio show was close to being over, it was time to leave. We had breakfast at Kindergarten, a hot kitchen cooked lunch, nap time and a snack. I usually went home around 6 p.m.

Going to Kindergarten was a fantastic experience and I had a marvelous time there. Our Kindergarten was very nature oriented, and we would have many outdoor adventures because a forest bordered the back of our building. It was a perfect setup for Easter because there were lots of places to hide the chocolate. On the property, we had two wooden tepees, a lodge house with pretend kitchen appliances and utensils, a huge sandbox, a garden, concrete picnic tables and lots of outside toys, e.g. tricycles, balls, chalkboards, scooters, etc.

I loved the tepees and the log cabin the most. One time I picked up some rocks near one of the tepees and kept banging them together until one broke in half. That rock had tiny white seashells embedded in it. It was the most amazing thing I had ever seen. Of course, I showed it to all my friends and they were equally fascinated. Eventually, one of the teachers got a hold of it and I never saw it again.

The log cabin was a lot of fun. It was huge! Now, it could have been an overstatement, especially since I was so small, but it certainly seemed huge at the time. The cabin had two or three windows, was equipped with a stove inside and general household items, and it all made a great setting for our version of "House of the Prairie" and Cowboys versus Indians. I always pretended to be a Native American because I thought they were much cooler and generally had more fun. After all, they were able to stay outside all the time and never had to go to school. They also had great clothes and war paint – you just couldn't beat that. Since my mom had such great sewing skills, she designed and created all my costumes for Fasching. My first choice was to be a Native American, of course. She made it out of those gray floor wash clothes and then attached tiny colorful beads all over it. It is still is my favorite costume. The only thing that didn't match was my short blond hair, but hey – you can't be too picky.

We had gymnastics in Kindergarten. Any excuse to move and jump around was a winner in my book. I didn't like sitting still because I got bored so easily. Some of the teachers did not appreciate that very much.

We also participated in plays and would perform in front of our parents. I acted in "Hansel and Gretel". I was so obsessed with it, that I learned every line in the story just in case someone forgot the words; which they did all the time. I think I was five years old then. My mom still talks about it, and apparently, everyone was amazed that I had memorized the whole thing. What can I say? I was committed!

Nap time was almost painful because we slept on plywood cots that were set up above the ground. No cushioning at all. We had a "nap supervisor" and I always got the evil eye from the woman with long black hair, because I never slept. She hated me, I'm certain of it. What can I say? I was not tired. It truly was my least favorite part of the day. Who wants to sleep in the middle of the day?! I never understood that concept at all.

On the upside, I got to hand out little blue pills before nap time started. They were supposed to be some sort of fluoride supplement. I just liked the minty taste of them and always sneaked a few extra ones for myself. I can't recall any negative side effects – I think. We brushed our teeth first, with the toothbrushes and toothpaste we had just for Kindergarten. It was all part of the "staying healthy campaign."

Snack time was worth looking forward to, because we usually had warm cocoa or Kindercoffee and a sweet treat.

Of course, we ate lunch as well. We all had lunch boxes made of leather. Mine was an orange color. I loved the smell of it. It was very comforting. My mom always asked me what I wanted to take and it usually was some sort of sandwich with salami or Teewurst. I was not raised to be a picky eater and I never complained, because I loved that kind of sandwich. Simple and delicious. By the way, we never put tomatoes or lettuce or mayo on our sandwiches. That's just weird.

During warm weather, we all had to hang our lunch boxes outside alongside the building. That made things easier when our parents came to pick us up – no need to go inside the building again. I used to stroll alongside the building to look at all the different lunch bags. Some of them had stickers on them with googly eyes and I thought it was the coolest thing ever and wondered who they might belong to.

People might think it must have been difficult to be in Kindergarten (Americans would consider it pre-school) all day, but I never thought of it that way. It was more like a daily educational playtime.

We had all kinds of activities there, including Fasching. That particular event was fun, merely because you could dress up as anything you wanted. It was sort of like Halloween in the United States. As mentioned earlier, my mom would make all my costumes, and she did a great job. They always looked store-bought. I got to be all kinds of characters during those years, including a devil, Rapunzel, a dwarf from Snow-white, and a Native American woman. Those were great times.

During Fasching, we always got to eat Berliner donuts. They were jelly filled, but there was always one that had a mustard filling. Yikes. Thankfully, I never got one of those.

During Easter, the teachers decorated the rooms very cheerfully with lots of pastel colors. There would be plastic Easter eggs hanging from tiny branches, and we were always included in the crafting of our own tiny Easter baskets.

As mentioned before, we had a huge forest behind the daycare facility. Therefore, our Easter egg hunt would always take place outside. I particularly remember one year after it had rained quite a lot. There were these tiny, thin, brownish mushrooms all over the forest floor. At some point, I placed myself in the midst of them with my Easter basket and not only started picking them, but actually eating them as well. So much for the supervision of the kids. Today I consider myself quite fortunate to not have acquired mushroom poisoning. I'm serious when I say that I was the luckiest kid at that moment. Apparently, I did not like the taste very much, because I don't recall any second helpings.

Christmas was always my favorite time, in Kindergarten and in general. It was always a big deal and we started with our decorations in early December. Most importantly, there was the Christmas calendar. I remember making our own. We would use a matchbox for each day. It was decorated, of course. You opened it every day and it would have a little tiny surprise inside. Nothing fancy...maybe a sticker or a piece of chocolate. I just thought it was charming and it really gave you something to look forward to every day.

We listened to Christmas music and would sing songs. As the holiday got closer, we would have special snack times. They arranged the tables into one long buffet. In the center, they put a big Gingerbread house that had a candle burning inside. There were smaller candles lit at several places on the table. Not one single child touched them; we just knew better than that. All the lights were turned off and only the candles lit up the room. It was so magical. We listened to German Christmas music, of course, and ate traditional, homemade Christmas cookies. The place was filled with "magic"; I loved the flickering candles-lights and the shadows it created on my friends' faces the walls. Since Russian fairy tales were among of my favorites, it truly felt like I was in a midst of a story when Christmas came around. Nothing and nobody could take the magical feeling away from me; it was oozing out of my every pore.

Of course, there were a lot of Christmas crafts as well - from snowflakes to homemade greeting cards to one of my favorite things, the edible Santa Claus. For this particular craft, I needed a red apple, a cotton ball, a walnut and some markers. I would color a face on the walnut, then glue to the bottom of the nut to the cotton ball so it would look like a beard and fluffy jacket collar. Then I attached the whole thing to the top of the red apple and voila! An edible Santa. This always made a great gift. I always loved giving; nothing put a bigger smile on my face than making someone else happy by giving them a present. All my gifts were homemade, but I poured my heart and soul in every crayon line, glue drop and ribbon. Seeing someone open one of my presents was as exciting as receiving one for myself. Christmas was and always will be exactly that for me – a chance to spread joy and warmth to everyone everywhere. It's not just presents, Santa Claus and decorations to me, it's a feeling – the absolute sum of joy, happiness and togetherness.

In addition to all the wonderful decorations, music and crafts, we also had a secret Santa come to visit us every year. He would have a present for each child. Of course, we couldn't just walk up to Santa and expect him to hand over the goods. Even as a small child, we knew what was expected of us. So, he would call your name and you had to go and stand in front of Santa. He would ask you a few questions, and then wanted to know what you would perform for him and the class. That was the moment you gave Santa a gift by singing a song or reciting a poem. If he liked it, you would get your present. He knew all the bad kids, and let me tell you, - there were no presents for them. They got some words from Santa instead, and maybe got away with a chocolate treat, but nothing wrapped in a box. Those kids knew what to do if they wanted a present the following year. There was no messing around with the German Santa Claus.

One year my dad was the one dressing up as Santa. I was very confused and excited at the same time. Is my dad Santa? No!! Impossible! He did not wear a red suit, but instead his green hunting outfit (without the rifle, of course). He never broke character, and I had to stand in front of him and recite a poem, just like all the other kids. I winked at him and smiled as I walked away. I was absolutely thrilled that my dad was our Santa Claus. He never talked about it, even after I got home that evening. I never mentioned it either, because I was afraid to diminish the magic of it all. I handled it as if it was my very own secret.

I loved the Weihnachtsmann so much that I'd cry when he left. It was never the actual presents that made the holiday special, even though they were always appreciated. It truly was about the

Christmas spirit and what it meant to just be together with friends and family, the smell of cookies, the Christmas markets, the oranges (if you were lucky enough to get some), the music, decorations, the Christmas tree, and just being home for three days and absolutely enjoying every minute of it.

Christmas Season

Let's just talk about St. Nicolaus for a minute. You might not have heard of him or when he comes to visit. December 6th has always been a special day for us kids because it meant a boot full of chocolate. Remember that we did not have Halloween, so, we certainly didn't have an enormous stash of candy and chocolate left over. But, when St. Nicolaus' Day approached, it was all about shining your boots. The shinier they were, the more chocolate you would get. Since I was eager to get a lot of chocolate, I volunteered to shine everyone's boots; especially my dad's, because they were the tallest. On the evening of December 5th, we put our shoes or boots in the foyer hoping to wake up to sweets and maybe a small gift. However, if you were bad in the days leading up to Sankt Nicolaus' Day, you might find a stick in your boot instead. As you can imagine, my brother and I made every attempt to get along together in the weeks before. Thankfully, it always worked out in our favor. One time, I received a sleigh! It was the best present ever! I was very proud of it. As far as I was concerned, snow could have come at any time.

Christmas at home had its own special charms. My dad regularly made a huge fuss over the Christmas tree, and now that I'm old enough, so do I. It must be genetic! It took us forever to find the perfect tree. When I say forever, I mean a minimum of three hours. Anything for the "perfect" tree. My dad is a hunter, so we would usually go into the forest of his hunting grounds to find the perfect tree. You have to understand that we wouldn't start this search a week or so before Christmas Eve, but the day before. It was usually snowing, and that gave the whole tree search some nice atmosphere, but when it started to get dark and we still had no tree, it was not so great anymore. Despite the difficulty, going out into nature with my dad was always very special to me. He was my hero and could do no wrong in my eyes. If it took all day to find the perfectly shaped tree, then that's just the way it was. It was funny, really. We would go through the woods and think we found *the* tree. So, then we walked around to look at it from every possible angle to figure out which side would be best for facing the wall and which side for facing the room. The shape had to be right, not too short, not too tall, not too wide, not too skinny, not ugly, and not crooked in any way because it would just cause all kinds of trouble with the tree stand, or - so I was told. Now you understand why the process took so long. We would have to check at least ten trees after covering at least forty acres of land. It was definitely an adventure. Then we would take the tree home and it would stand in the basement or garage for about twenty-four hours to dry a bit and open up.

On Christmas Eve, he would bring the tree into the house and set it up. Then another huge and exacting project began – actually decorating the tree. You could never just decorate it any way you wanted. First, the lights were hung in the perfect places from top to bottom, never the other way around. Once this was completed, we could start with the ornaments. We had to lay them out according to size. The big ones had to go on the bottom of the tree and the smaller ones towards the top. After that was done, we would have a few other ornaments here and there, but not too many, because it's too distracting. As far as the very top of the tree is concerned, my dad always puts up some fancy pointy thing. It looked like a tousle or something, but in a pretty gold or silver color. To give the tree its final touch, we were allowed to strategically place the "Lametta" (tinsel) on the tree. We were coached by my dad all along the way to assure perfect distribution. Then he would step back a bit to better inspect it. Once he was satisfied, he turned the lights on. Then it was officially Christmas! I have to admit that I truly loved the whole ordeal. It is so memorable and unique to him. He brainwashed me and now I can't help but do the same thing when I put up a Christmas tree. He'd be so proud.

My mom was and still is the master chef and baker. We would make Christmas cookies together and bake like there was no tomorrow.

We would listen to Christmas music and sing our hearts out. I didn't say we could carry a tune, but that made it even more fun. I would always go a bit overboard with my cookie decorations, but it was a holiday and in my mind, it had to be colorful all around. My mom would cook the Christmas goose or duck for the main meal with red cabbage, Brussels sprouts or green vegetables with potatoes. Christmas was and still is a three-day event. Christmas Eve, we would have potato salad and Bockwurst. Christmas day was the goose or duck, and on Boxing Day (2nd Christmas day) we have another big meal. Delicious!

Also, my mom was extremely creative - she would spread the Christmas spirit all through the house by putting up window decorations and presenting the homemade wreath in the center of the table with four candles on it; one for each week of Advent prior to the Christmas Eve. The candles were always red, big and fat. Not only was it a cozy environment, but it would help count down the weeks until the big day. Of course, we also had a Christmas countdown calendar. One year we had a huge paper one in the kitchen next to the table. No chocolate, but a great winter scene that made me want to be part of it. As we got older, we had the calendars with the chocolate in each window. It was really hard to not cheat and harvest the chocolate from days yet to come. My brother usually did, but I truly wanted that piece of chocolate every single day! My mom would also teach me how to make paper stars and snowflakes, but one of my most favorite things she did was paint our window. You never got a better Christmas view than that. One year it was a big snow scene with falling flakes and a big happy snowman. The next it was a huge smiling Santa Claus with a sack full of presents.

When it was time for presents Christmas Eve (usually around 6p.m.) my parents sent my brother and me to our room. We were not allowed to come out until they said we could. We placed ourselves right in front of our door and tried to sneak a peek at the stuff they were carrying from their hiding places to the tree. So exciting! We could never see anything, but their feet. Once they would call us, we'd nearly trample each other.

The family room was lit up with the lights from the Christmas tree and the candles flickering in the wreath on the coffee table. It created a perfect setting for opening gifts with music playing in the background. We would never face a mountain of presents or anything even close to that. We would usually get two presents each. One was always practical, like a sweater or pants. Another was sometimes a toy, but more often a book. I always loved my book, because it was usually one you couldn't just get in any bookstore. It was specially ordered by my mom who knew the owner of the bookstore. The most important item under the tree was the Christmas plate. Mine was shaped like a star and my brother's was round. It would have an orange, mandarins, walnuts, hazelnuts and chocolate on it. Oranges were very rare. They were rationed, distributed in precise amounts to each family, one pound of oranges, which meant about 5 to 6 pieces, and about one pound of mandarins. That was why those Christmas plates were so eagerly anticipated. There were always things my brother and I traded because we liked some things more than others. I would spend all holiday sitting next to my tin plate and reading my book beside to the lit Christmas tree. It was the greatest thing to me and I was never disappointed - as long as I had my chocolate Santa Claus!

Throughout the holiday we would light all four candles on the wreath, burnt incense in the "Raeuchermaennchen" and light the candle in the gingerbread house. Every year they aired my favorite show on our one TV channel - "Weihnachten in Familie". I loved it, and I still have the music on vinyl to listen to every Christmas. We played cards and board games. It was quality family time

Another great part of Christmas is the Christmas markets (Weihnachtsmarkt). All the bigger cities usually had one. My favorite was and still is in Berlin at the Alexanderplatz. Already big and beautiful, it seemed even more amazing to a little person like me. I was always excited when my mom took me to the Christmas market. First of all, it was a chance to get a head start by reminding Santa Claus that I had been really good that year, and secondly, I got to have chestnuts and my most favorite thing, - a big, red candy apple! I lived for that stuff. My face would be all red and sticky, but it was worth the mess every single time. I'm sure my mom was of a different about that. Meeting the

Weihnachtsmann on the market was a bit easier than other places because you didn't have to have a poem or song in your back pocket. He'd just asked a couple questions and then you got your piece of chocolate. There were some rides at the market as well, and the best time to go, was at night or just when it was getting dark. There were lights and Christmas music everywhere, and all sorts of delicious smells that you only experience during the Christmas holiday. I'll bet my heart skipped a beat because I was so thrilled to be there. If my mom took me twice or more I had the same jubilant feeling every time.

It wasn't Christmas unless you visited the market at least once. When we went as a family, my parents always got a cup of Gluehwein; a spiced red wine heated just below the boiling point. It smelled so good. With a hot cup in one hand and a Bratwurst in the other, it couldn't get much better. It was usually so cold and windy that I got to sneak an occasional sip of the hot wine as well. I got cozy pretty quickly after that. I usually stuck with my hot chocolate and whipped cream. As a child, the Christmas Market was the equivalent of living in your own fairy tale. There were vendors everywhere selling traditional ornaments made out of blown glass or wood, candles, wreaths, scarfs, gloves, and of course different foods. An absolute must-have were the gingerbread hearts. They came in all shapes and sizes with different designs and statements or names on them. You never had to find a space in your pockets either, because they were on a string and you could just hang them around your neck. The noise of the bumper cars, the merry-go-around, Christmas music, people talking and laughing combined with all the different colored lights and holiday scents in the air made the entire event spellbinding with a strangely pleasant side of vertigo. I was never ready for the fun to end, and when it was finally time to go, I was keen to go back sooner rather than later.

Easter

What another great holiday, full of tasty chocolate eggs and chocolate bunnies! Easter was always fun, and started on the Friday prior (Karfreitag). My mom decorated the house with Easter ornaments a week ahead of time. My dad would bring home young twigs from the birch tree and we would put them into a big floor vase. We hung little wooden Easter ornaments and funky looking yellow plastic chicks on the thin branches to cheer up the whole room. Later, when we bought a house, we would decorate the outdoor area as well – the smaller trees and the forsythia bushes were adorned with colorful plastic eggs. Easter Sunday was totally awesome. My dad made a special breakfast with hot cocoa and German pancakes. Soon afterwards, my brother and I would have to go outside and start our hunt for all the goodies. My dad was an absolute expert at hiding the Easter candy. He would put it inside the dog house (with the dog still in it), in the trees, inside the watering can, and in all sorts of unexpected nooks and crannies. One year, he did such a fantastic job that even he couldn't find that one chocolate bunny we were missing. He thought for sure he hid it inside the long, tall pine bush in the front yard, but we could not recover it. Then, about four months later, while he was watering the yard, he sprayed that particular pine bush – and the chocolate bunny flew out!

The rest of the Easter holiday we spent just eating chocolate and candy and playing with friends.

My dad would tell us about times when he was little and had to get a bucket of water from the well early on Easter morning. Thankfully, we had no well close by to imitate that custom.

In Kindergarten and later in the early school years, we always made our own Easter baskets with leftover plastic containers. We filled it with dirt and grass seeds. Then we would make this paper rabbit and glue it to the container. On Easter week, the teachers placed colored boiled eggs inside of it to take home. It was all very cheery and springy.

Speaking of colored eggs, - my mom would make us blow the egg whites and yolks out with a straw. I have never been that dizzy in my life. It's worse than blowing up those tiny balloons that clowns never seem to have problems with. It was extremely hard because the stuff is not easy to blow out of a tiny hole and you couldn't break the egg or you would have to start all over again. After the torturous preparation, we got to decorate the eggshells with paint and melted candle wax. This way we were able to keep our own artwork for years to come and brag about it.

New Year's

We call this holiday Silvester, (in honor of Pope Silvester), and it is always a big party. I looked forward to it every year. We either had people come over to our apartment or we would go to the neighbors'. The adults would sit around and talk, dance to their favorite songs, and drink wine, champagne or beer, and we kids just did all the things we were not allowed to do any other time of the year, ... things like jumping on the bed, being much too loud, and pretending we can play all available musical instruments really well. Ouch!

Fireworks were a big deal among the people I knew. You could only purchase them for private use from December 27 to December 30. Originally, the loud noises at midnight were to ward off evil spirits back in the medieval times, but when I was growing up it was for pure fun and enjoyment, kicking off the New Year with a big bang.

We either had loud music in the background or watched some New Year's entertainment on the TV. They had a huge clock on stage which would eventually give the countdown to midnight.

Some of the "good luck" foods we surrounded ourselves with were Sauerkraut, carp or herring, and a variety of marzipan treats in the shapes of pigs, four-leaf clovers, mushrooms and ladybugs. Yes, we were and still are quite the superstitious bunch. A big crowd pleaser and must-have at any party was the "Bowle" – basically a punch created from juice, alcohol and fruit. There was a non-alcoholic version for the kids.

We also had a wide variety of party games. I especially loved the table fireworks. They either had confetti, a puzzle, or little toys inside. Another of my favorite activities was Bleigießen. Essentially, you had several lead pieces that were shaped like a pig, a bell, a hat, etc.; all considered good luck symbols. You needed a big bowl of cold water, an old metal spoon and a candle. Then you had to choose your lead piece, put it on the spoon and hold it over the candle until the lead melted. Once that happened, you poured the liquid lead into the water where it would cool into all sorts of shapes. Then the fun part was figuring out what on earth you had created! Everyone would chime in to identify the mysterious shape. Depending on what it was (a flower, a bird, a stick, a dragon, etc.); it would predict your fortune for the New Year. I guess, it was our version of a Chinese fortune cookie; except this one was inedible.

When I was very young, I'd fall asleep in the course of the evening, but my parents would wake me up right before midnight so I could be part of the celebration.

At midnight, the adults would toast "Guten Rutsch" ("have a good slide") with champagne, and the kids had some sort of sparkling juice. Then everyone would go outside to set off rockets and colorful fireworks. It was quite a display, and I loved the entire show!! It seemed to go on forever, and after some time, all you could see was the smoky fog from the fireworks.

Erntedankfest (Harvest Fest)

This festival was usually held in late September or early October to celebrate the end of the harvest season. It was not a huge event, but big enough to be worth anticipating every autumn. Somewhere in town, they would set up tables, a grill station, and a live band.

Everyone would come together just to talk, eat and drink. As kids, it was especially fun because we got to run around, play with friends, eat lots of food and play games. Basically, people would talk about the harvest of that particular year, the weather and events to come.

May Day (May 1st)

Now that's a day I looked forward to every year. It always started with a huge bonfire the night before (Walpurgisnacht). I would gather with my friends and just enjoy not only the time apart from our parents, but the enormous fire as well. No worries; there were always two to three fire trucks close by. It was always a good excuse to stay out late, especially considering that we would usually stay until the fire burnt out. There was music, food, and lots of people.

The next morning, everyone got together again at the soccer field. Naturally there were soccer games for of different age groups all day, some exercise program for everyone, and lots of games. We did have a Maypole, but not the one you dance around. (We weren't in Bavaria, after all). On the very top of the pole was a ring from which all kind of toys would hang. In order to pick one, you had to climb to the top of the pole. First come, first served. They generally did not have duplicate toys, so you stood in line hoping nobody picked the one toy you were going for. That's where my brother usually came in handy. He'd climb up and then give me his toy later (after I got my own). So, I usually ended up with two toys that day. Success!!

They consistently had great food, music, and games. One game that received a lot of attention from kids and adults alike was the target shooting station. There we would shoot at plastic pieces to have flowers fall off the wall. They also had a bullseye game, the more points you collected, the more likely it was for you to win the grand prize. My mom won the grand prize once, which turned out to be a real, live piglet. How awesome! My dad was not as thrilled as I was, of course. When my parents picked up the piglet the next morning, they were debating what to do with it. I decided that it needed a name first of all, and the name was: Otto. I loved the pig and really wanted to keep it. My dad wasn't so sure.

Next thing I knew, my dad was working for hours in the garage. When I felt it was an appropriate time to check on him, I discovered that he had built a pig sty!! I was overjoyed. Otto was happy, too. He was running around in his new home and loving all the attention. Otto was very spoiled. He got all kinds of foods and scraps. He grew very fast and eventually reached 500kg. I would brush him, only to feel his big foot standing on mine. I would push him to the side and discipline him like an 8-year-old girl would. I loved that pig. I would even sit on him. As I've said, I was a tiny thing, and he was literally the biggest pig I had ever laid eyes on.

Eventually, the sad day we didn't like thinking about arrived; a big butcher truck pulled up to the house and Otto was loaded up. He kicked and squealed so loudly, I wanted to cry. I never saw him again, and my mom refused to buy pork for an entire month out of fear we'd eat our own pig. We were left with an empty pig sty full of fond memories of Otto.

To make up for the loss, my dad bought three more piglets. They were a funny bunch, always sticking together and getting in trouble. One day after school, when I fed them, they walked straight out of the pig sty into the yard! Being by myself, and fearing my father's reaction if he found out, I knew I had to get them back into the garage and into their pig sty as soon as possible. That was not an easy task. After what seemed like hours, I eventually gathered them one by one. The last two I literally sat on and guided them back inside the garage. It was stressful, yet fun at the same time! Pigs are so funny and smart, but they sure are sneaky.

Oh, my parents never found out about that particular escapade (at least, until they read this story).

One other very enjoyable activity was the lantern parade for kids. Once it was dark, the kids grouped together and walked through the city with lit lanterns. I only remember doing this when we lived in the city, but it was very peaceful and magical. We each had our own lantern made of plastic in different colors that were lit with a candle inside. I believe mine was either orange or blue. I do not recall what the exact starting and ending points where of the parade itself, but remember walking from the school to the soccer field when we were living in the country. Mainly what I can picture in my mind is the delight of being able to be outside in the dark while the rest of the world settling down for a restful night of sleep. I almost felt like our small group were the only people roaming around under a belly of the night sky filled with stars; it was as if the world stood still for just a moment.

While walking on the sidewalks, we sang the Lantern song; on and off:

Kinderlieder - Ich geh' mit meiner Laterne

Ich gehe mit meiner Laterne und meine Laterne mit mir.

Da oben leuchten die Sterne, hier unten leuchten wir.

Ein Lichtermeer zu Martins Ehr, Rabimmel, Rabammel, Rabumm.

Ein Lichtermeer zu Martins Ehr, Rabimmel, Rabammel, Rabumm.

Ich gehe mit meiner Laterne und meine Laterne mit mir.

Da oben leuchten die Sterne, hier unten leuchten wir.

Der Martinsmann, der zieht voran. Rabimmel, Rabammel, Rabumm.

Der Martinsmann, der zieht voran. Rabimmel, Rabammel, Rabumm.

Ich gehe mit meiner Laterne und meine Laterne mit mir.

Da oben leuchten die Sterne, hier unten leuchten wir.

Wie schön das klingt, wenn jeder singt. Rabimmel, Rabammel, Rabumm.

Wie schön das klingt, wenn jeder singt. Rabimmel, Rabammel, Rabumm.

Children's songs - I'm going with my lantern

I go with my lantern and my lantern with me.

The stars glow above, here we shine.

A sea of lights to Martins Ehr, Rabimmel, Rabammel, Rabumm.

A sea of lights to Martins Ehr, Rabimmel, Rabammel, Rabumm.

I go with my lantern and my lantern with me.

The stars glow above, here we shine.

The Martinsmann, who is moving forward. Rabim, Rabbi, Rabum.

The Martinsmann, who is moving forward.
Rabim, Rabbi, Rabum.

I go with my lantern and my lantern with me.

The stars glow above, here we shine.

How beautiful that sounds when everyone sings.
Rabim, Rabbi, Rabum.

How beautiful that sounds when everyone sings.
Rabim, Rabbi, Rabum.

Transportation

We walked everywhere. A car was definitely not
our main means of transportation, nor was it for
most people. On the other hand, public
transportation was great and easily accessible.
Buses, trolleys, trains, city trains,
undergrounds...we had it all. No planes, though.
Flying was also not a means of transportation we
were privileged enough to enjoy. I don't think I
ever even saw a plane; at least not a commercial
one. I personally got motion sick very quickly
and didn't quite enjoy public transportation as

much as other people. I did like the trains, though, as long as I was facing the direction we were going and if I was allowed to open the window to stick my head out.

Apparently, in addition to my motion sickness I also had a side of claustrophobia. Now, it makes complete sense to me; but back then I always wondered why my mom and I got off the trolley just to see it move past us going the same direction we were going.

The train and trolley were not all bad, though; I loved punching the tickets. The trolley, had especially interesting punching patterns, usually a variety of punch holes which I might have overdone a few times. It did have a date stamp on it, (probably several) after I had finished with it. Looking back, my mom was very patient letting me punch the same ticket over and over again without taking it away from me. I know for a fact that my dad would have ripped it out of my hand in no time.

We also used our bicycles all the time. If it was too far to walk, or you didn't necessarily want to use public transportation, you rode your bike. It also was quite convenient for grocery shopping, because instead of carrying the bags in your hands, you could hang or strap them to your bike. Even the elderly used their bikes for carrying their groceries home.

My dad owned a motorcycle and I had been in love with it ever since I got to ride on it with him. I had a pair of really cool fuzzy plastic goggles in a tiger print and thought I was the coolest kid in town. On the good days, he let me sit in front of him and I felt like I was in charge! It was so exhilarating! Any chance I got, I would go with him just for the ride, even if it was to the most boring or annoying places; like the hardware store for instance. When we still lived in the apartment, he would park it right outside the entrance. When he was not looking, I would sit on it and pretend I was riding all over the world, or at least the part of it I knew, I didn't quite know what the "whole" world really meant at that time. I was only five.

Diet & Food in general

We Germans love our bread, and that's pretty much what we ate the most of, second only to potatoes. We had white bread or rolls with marmalade, plum spread, honey, or chocolate spread for breakfast. Sandwiches for lunch were made with dark bread and topped with meat spread or salami without any complicated condiments. In Kindergarten or school, we had the opportunity to get hot lunches. For dinner, we had dark bread with sausages, cheese or eggs. Of course, we ate fruit as well, just not anything exotic. So, it was whatever was locally in season - apples, strawberries, currants, blackberries, blueberries, plums, cherries, gooseberries or pears. Never bananas or pineapples or anything else fancy or "foreign".

My mom would make stew on Saturdays and a meat-potato-vegetable dish on Sundays. That might sound boring, but it wasn't. Every weekend was a different meal, and the leftovers would always lead to an entirely new meal creation.

At 3pm it was hot chocolate or hot tea time for the kids or coffee for the adults. We would generally have a piece of cake or pie with it. If you didn't have that, it was bread with some type of sweet spread.

Why do we love bread? We have great bakeries! They would have fresh bread and rolls ready at 6a.m. every day. My mom would consistently ask me if I wanted to go to the bakery with her. I always accepted not because I wanted to get some sweet dessert, but I got to have a roll! My favorite ones were sourdough or poppy seed rolls. I was in heaven, and would savor my roll of choice every single time. My mom had company and I had my piece of bread as an incentive to walk with her. We were both happy. I didn't care that I had to walk 2 miles to get there. The reward was always worth it to me. It was basically the equivalent of today's candy bar at the checkout aisle.

All our food was essentially made from scratch. There were no ready to cook meals like TV dinners or boxed macaroni & cheese. We didn't even have yogurt in fancy cups. You had to buy the plain yogurt in glass bottles, take it home to add sugar and the fruit you had available that time of the year. Then you washed the bottle and took it back to the store for a small refund. We were all about recycling. Nothing got wasted. We hardly had any trash, because you bought mostly everything in its original state. Everything came in glass bottles, jars or tetra cartons. No pre-cooked frozen foods or boxed foods.

That's hard to imagine for some people, but it's just the way it was and it never seemed an inconvenience to anybody. If you don't know it to be any other way, you couldn't actually miss it or complain. Even elderly people walked to the store with their bicycles. There were no plastic bags, but netted or cotton bags. Lots of people used actual baskets. No waste.

We had a grocery store in town that had exactly four aisles. One was for paper products and school supplies, one for laundry stuff and shoe polishes, etc., an aisle for chocolate, cookies, and pretzels, and one aisle for cake mixes and baby food. There was a refrigerated food section, too - well, the refrigerator section was about the size of two American home refrigerators. The frozen section, if that's what you want to call it, was as big as a regular deep freezer and it was mostly empty. There were never any advertisements because we had no sales or ads. Whatever was in the store is what you could buy. If someone said they had chocolate spread and you wanted it, you had to race to the store, but it was probably all gone by the time you got there. It was like that with most things. Huge lines formed in the hope that they could get something "different" for a change. My mom would tell my brother and me to go to the store early in the morning to stand in line at the butcher. Then she would come about 2 hours later and meet us in line to just get some sausages and lunch meat, if they still had it by then. Saving a spot in the line was always an important job, because without someone doing it, there was no chance of having the meat you wanted on the table for the weekend lunches. So, if that ever happened, you'd have to be really creative. Trust me, every East German woman was a secret iron chef. My mom could make super tasty dishes out of thin air!

People who lived in the country or owned a garden property would usually grow much of their own produce, especially fruit. I'd say most people had apple or pear trees, cherry trees and lots of berry bushes and grapevines. We had three types of current bushes and two different gooseberry bushes. Oh, how I loved those gooseberries. They were just so delicious and addictive. Our Rottweiler liked them, too. I'm not sure how he got around all the thorns on the bush, but he seemed to have a true talent.

I was given my own garden space when I was around eight years old. This gift of temporary produce property made me incredibly happy. It was my shining moment to put all my acquired garden skills to use. After all, I tended to the garden we had in Kindergarten on a daily basis. Additionally, I was a pretty good observer and apprentice gardener for my dad. He showed me my space and told me that I could grow whatever I wanted there. He made it perfectly clear that it was 100% my responsibility to take care of my crops and that he would not renew my garden space lease the following year if I didn't give enough of my time to the plants. My crop of choice was carrots, of course!! I loved carrots, and I made sure to grow plenty of them. Who needs a fake tan when you can just eat carrots and turn orange?! Oh yes, I was orange. My eyesight is still great.

Then there were our mushroom outings. Ever since I could remember, towards the end of summer my parents would take us to gather mushrooms in the forest. We only picked the ones that could be 100% recognized with your eyes closed. I loved picking them. It was so much fun running around and gathering as many as possible and, of course, it was a great learning experience as well. When we moved to the house in the country, my brother and I would go picking by ourselves. We would pick the ones we were familiar with, and then some other ones that we thought were edible. My dad would always check the questionable ones, of course. We never had mushroom poisoning! One year, when my brother and I were out again, we were on our way home with empty baskets after a disappointing hunt when we stumbled across a big tree that stood at the very end of the road. We passed the tree all the time but had never seen the mushrooms. We could hardly believe our eyes - a huge assembly of big fat white champignons. It was like we struck gold. We were literally skipping home to show off our find. That never happened again, but it was certainly a grand experience, and great for storytelling.

Now, you might think that after all the gathering of the mushrooms that I could hardly wait to eat them. I loved the smell in the air when my mom was cooking them, but I didn't like to eat them very much. I'm not even sure why. My portion shrank every time we ate them. Every time, I'd tell myself "this time I will like them for sure." It didn't happen. After the first bite, I thought, "this is good," then after the second bite I realized, "no, I can't do it!" How disappointing! Fortunately, I grew to like them as I got older. Until then, I just stuck with picking the mushrooms.

We also picked wild berries. Starting around May, we were able to go into the woods and collect wild strawberries, blueberries, and raspberries. This was certainly more fun and more rewarding than mushrooms because you got to eat the fruit while you were picking them. Occasionally, we would ride our bikes further away to the old roads from WWII that had fruit trees lined up on both sides of the street. Usually, it was either cherry or apple trees. I remember when I first came across those roads. I must have been around eight or nine years old. I thought it strange at first that there were fruit trees along the road instead of "regular" trees, but my parents told me how they got there and I just accepted it for what it was. Since they didn't belong to anyone, in particular, we were able to pick the fruit.

Now, you know we love our bread, but we also love potatoes. You could buy potatoes in the grocery store, but that was rarely necessary once we started living in the country. Once a year, we had 250 kg (about 550 lbs.) of potatoes delivered directly to our basement. I'm not sure if my dad built the big metal potato storage unit or if it already existed in the house, but it was quite big and tall, standing against the wall. The sheer number of potatoes was a bit shocking for me at first, because this meant that as a family of four we consumed a lot of spuds in just one year. We did not turn them into French fries, but rather boiled them for a wide variety of dishes. We had a small orange basket of potatoes in the bathroom. Then, as we ran out, I would go down to the basement and refill it. It was quite efficient.

Health Check before entering school

I have to admit that I don't look back on this time fondly. Before entering first grade, the pediatrician came to Kindergarten to do a health check. Since I had a history of being sick with high fevers, I was able to go to my own pediatrician for my check-up. Unlucky me, I was sent to the hospital for further testing. The children's hospital was about ten miles from home. When you are five or six years old, that is really far away.

I stayed there for two weeks, and every day the nurse would give me some type of necklace that had a certain colored piece of plastic hanging from it. The color determined if I could eat or drink that morning or not. I had to get a lot of testing done and I can't remember much of it. I often felt and wandered the halls at night because I couldn't sleep. It was very quiet in the hospital, and the door to my room was constantly left open. I'm not sure why. Maybe it was easier for the charge nurse to check on us. I shared a room with one other person, but don't remember her or him. All I noticed was that my roommate received a lot of visitors, unlike me.

The hallway lights were usually dimmed at night, and only certain rooms seemed to have normal lighting; the nurse offices, I guessed. One night when I was walking the halls, I heard a nurse talking softly in the distance. So, I got closer to the room she was in. I peeked around the open door and saw a child lying on the table with all sorts of wires, tubes and other things attached to it next to a big medical machine. It was very surreal, and I remember just standing there in the dark hallway staring at the scene in front of me. Then the nurse saw me and, surprised, she took my hand and walked me back to my room. I think I was on a watch list after that night, because I would get in so much trouble every time I left my bed. The nurse even yelled at me when I walked to the bathroom directly across the hall. As you can imagine, she was not my favorite person.

Then one day I was able to go home. I was very eager to leave that place. The attending physician decided to give me a medication to go home with. Apparently, the medication was supposed to help me with a concern regarding my kidneys.

My mom took me to the grocery store after we got home and I was able to pick out ice cream for myself. I loved ice cream and picked my favorite cone; vanilla dipped in chocolate. I can still remember skipping on the way home from the store. The grass was green, it was a nice sunny summer day and I was waving to my friend, Rene', on the way into the apartment building. I was so happy to be home. When it was time for bed, my mom gave me the medication as instructed by the doctor. It was a small, yellow pill and I didn't like it at all. I can still remember the bitter taste in my mouth. Then I went to bed, only to find myself in the hospital again when I woke up.

It was quite frightening and confusing. I had no idea how I got there, or why I was back. It turned out that I had a severe reaction to the medication. Due to this allergic reaction, further testing was conducted and it was discovered that I had a hole between two chambers of my heart. Apparently, this should have been repaired shortly after I was born, but obviously, that had not happened.

Unfortunately, I was in the hospital for another two weeks. As mentioned before, I did not receive any visitors. My parents visited me only once, right after I was readmitted. I couldn't blame them; they didn't have a car and were both working full-time. On the day they did come to visit, we took a walk outside and I recall the breeze blowing that day, making the trees sway back and forth. It was a sunny day.

One day I received a big fat envelope. It was from my Kindergarten class. Each of my friends drew a picture for me and wished me well. I was so happy to be thought of and, best of all, there was a big bar of chocolate in it just for me. I can only imagine my big toothy smile at the sight of it. I loved chocolate!!!

After another two weeks in the hospital, my parents came to pick me up again. I was excited but also anxious going home. I guess, I wasn't sure if I would have to go back again or not. Thankfully, that was the last time I was there, but I had years of cardiology visits and testing ahead of me. The good news: no more medications for me!

The bad news: I was told to not exert myself physically; meaning no running, jumping, or anything that would get my heart rate up. This would cause all sorts of disappointment in school for me later on, especially in gym class.

School

Getting into school was a big deal. First grade was really special. They actually had an entire day set up for it. It was always a Saturday. You got to wear your fancy clothes and had your brand-new book bag filled with school supplies. That was not all. We also received big paper cones filled with neat school things and chocolate. Let me tell you, it was not just some regular cone. It was huge. It was about as tall as I was, or at least it definitely hit my shoulder. It was top heavy because of its shape, and you really had to balance it. It was quite a tricky thing for a first-grader to do. Friends and family were taking pictures of everything. You got to meet the people in your class, your teacher, and you found out where your seat was for the school year. I was in the front row and sat next to a guy who had huge glasses and big ears! That was not so bad, but he was really annoying and always got me in trouble. One time he would just not stop talking to me in class and I became angry and raised my voice at him. Then my teacher came over and pulled me off my seat by my ear. That was painful. To top it, I had to face the wall for the rest of the class. As you might guess, I did not like that teacher or my table mate.

Every class had two people assigned to get the milk crate. Each class-room would order milk either white or chocolate milk. I loved chocolate milk, but didn't get to order it very often. You had to shake it really well because the chocolate always settled on the bottom of the glass bottle.

We had school on every day, but Sunday. We went to school on Saturdays for about four hours, and then went home just in time for lunch. That might seem cruel, but that's how we grew up and it was not unusual for any of us. We didn't know any other way.

I loved school, but I especially loved the very first day of a school year, because everything was new - your books, papers without any writing on it, new pencils, ink pens, erasers, paint and colored pencils. When I got my new books, I generally looked through all the pages to find out what we would learn that particular year. Of course, I didn't understand it, but it sure looked interesting.

School books were an entire drama in themselves. The school would send a list home with all the books you would need for the upcoming year. The problem was that everyone got a list, and you'd see everyone in line at the grocery store hoping to receive the same books. Don't ask me why there was such a shortage, but I was always very worried that I wouldn't get all my books. My brother was never worried, of course. He didn't like school very much. So, while I was standing in line, I got a great look at all the notebooks and school supplies and wondered if I was able to buy certain items that I really wanted. Once I got home, I spread all my stuff over the entire floor and just took it all in, all the things I would have to carry around with me that entire school year. Then I started to put my name on everything. To me, that was just part of getting ready, even if summer vacation had just started. I always wanted a head start, just in case. I think my book bag was pretty much packed, perfectly organized and ready to go only a week after the school year was done. I was so nerdy. Some people will understand.

When you entered first grade, you were sort of sworn in to be a Young Pioneer. Membership in this group was voluntary, but certainly highly encouraged since it was the country's opportunity to teach you all lessons regarding its government, thinking and following certain rules. It wasn't really all that bad, but that's just my personal take on it. I loved the uniform, (a white shirt with the emblem on the left sleeve, blue pants, skirts and a cap, as well as a blue necktie,) and I felt "official." The slogan of the Young Pioneers was "For peace and socialism be ready – always ready!" We received our little membership pass that laid out our main goals and rules; for example, Young Pioneers love peace, the GDR, their parents, and they respect all working people, love to sing, dance, and play, exercise and keep their bodies clean and healthy.

In fourth grade, you graduated to become a Thaelmann Pioneer and received a red necktie. Ernst Thaelmann was the leader of the Communist party in Germany and was executed in the Buchenwald concentration camp. Every

Wednesday was Pioniertreffen (pioneer meeting). It was usually in the afternoon for about two hours and took place in the school. During those meetings, we would usually do some type of art project, sing and plan some type of fundraising to collect money for children in Africa. We would then use the money to buy books and school supplies and send them a package at least once a year. There was also the individual group in each class. You had the group leader, usually a teacher, and representatives for a certain part of the committee. All students voted for the person in charge of the particular position. I was voted to be the Treasurer of our class and handled all the monies. I was very excited and was proud of myself and the responsibilities that were given to me.

At the beginning of class in the morning, the student whose turn it was had to go to the front and tell everyone else to stand up. Then the student would salute by raising the right hand and putting it on top of his or her head (thumb to point to the forehead, and the pinky pointed to the sky) and tell the teacher if everyone was present or report who was absent. After that, the student had to turn towards the class again and say: "Seid bereit!" (Be prepared!) And the class had to answer: "Immer bereit!" (Always be prepared). Then everyone sat down and the class officially started.

Being a Pioneer was overall pretty cool - the whole uniform thing was annoying at times, but I kind of always liked it. After all, the uniform was blue, my favorite color at the time. I would have hated red or green or something. We didn't wear it all the time, of course; mostly for special events or holidays. The schools also distributed two types of magazines to young pioneers and the youth in general: the Trommel magazine and the ABC-Zeitschrift. As a smaller child, I loved reading and reviewing the Froesi magazine. It was a great magazine for kids, and always had stories, riddles, puzzles and the occasional contest. One time I won a contest and, as you can imagine, I was thrilled. I won colored pens and paint. It was certainly a highlight of my childhood.

We often seemed to have some kind of special event coming up in school. Of course, nobody would pay for that but us. In order to collect money, we would go on the big recycle mission. That might not sound too exciting, but recycling was not only the right thing to do, it was a lucrative business. Our class would split into individual groups and pick a week to go on the "recycling hunt." I usually had a least two other friends with me and we would get my dad's big trailer. Then we would push it to every single house and apartment building in town. We rang every doorbell and asked for every item that was to be recycled, --newspapers, glasses, bottles. Nothing could be broken, because it was not worth anything then. You had to hurry, because these missions usually happened at the same time other classes were trying to make money as well. First come, first served. There was serious competition, and you literally had to run with your trailer or make one person of the group the runner to make sure he or she would get to the next house first. We were basically cleaning people's houses. Elderly people were always so happy that we would collect those things. Then they didn't have to worry about it. We got some major exercise, pushing the trailer, lifting, moving, running up steps and down again. Of course, after we had hopefully filled the trailer to the top, we still had to take everything to the recycling station. It was located near the train station and looked like a shed. It was a very small room with a big scale on the ground in the corner and a counter with two people behind it. We would carefully put our bottles, jars and any other glass containers on the counter. The people who worked there would sort it by color first and then count everything. The paper had to be placed on the scale and we hoped it would be very heavy. Then they put all the information down on the receipt and handed it over to us. There you were able to check all the items and then get your money. I think the most we ever received for one of those "hunts" was about 15 Marks. That was a total jackpot for us! Bottles were like gold - free money, really. I remember walking home from school so many times looking for shiny things in the grass. Then, when I thought I saw a bottle, I'd keep my fingers crossed hoping it was not broken, because that would just be awful and worthless.

There were no real jobs for kids, - so we really counted on recycling throughout the year. Later in the summer, I'd help pick potatoes on fields or pick up haystacks.

One time I wanted to get some flowers for my mom for Mother's Day and didn't have any money. So, I decided to go to the greenhouse in town and ask the person who owned it if she needed help watering all the plants inside the glasshouse. In exchange, I wanted a little tiny flowerpot for my mom. It was a done deal, and I was able to give my mom something cheerful. So, every day I would ride my bike into the center of town to the flower shops and greenhouses to water the flowers and other plants. I did this for about one week. At the end of it, I was able to pick a small flower pot of my choice as payment. I was so proud of myself, and enjoyed a great feeling of accomplishment. Being able to give something to my mom, after I worked for it, made it extra special.

Another way to make money for our class was by holding a bake sale at recess. I'm sure you had your own share of bake sales, but I'm talking about the really tasty ones. These goodies were all made from scratch with lots of love and pride. We'd decide on the day and the cake or cookies each person would bring to make sure there were no doubles. My favorite was LPG Kuchen (chocolate cake with vanilla pudding cream and chocolate ganache on top) and Papageienkuchen (pound cake with different food colorings - like a tie dye only more organized). I loved bake sales! I would always go for seconds and thirds, after first checking with my friends to make sure what was left was worth the speed trip down the hallway. There were never any leftovers. It looked like an out of this world invasion happened and the aliens took all the goods but left crumbs behind. Nobody ever missed the bake sale.

Speaking of food, let's talk about school lunch. Some people might not think fondly of their school lunches and mean lunch ladies, but I truly looked forward to lunch. I could always smell delicious aromas from the time I arrived at school in the morning. There was always a huge mountain of potatoes in front of the kitchen, potatoes that were peeled by hands every day! Eventually I could anticipate the weekly menu, but it was fun to guess what was cooking that day. The lunch cost 5.50 Marks for two weeks. My parents made sure I had my Essengeld (lunch money) on time. There was a joke about some ugly blue and white converse-like sneakers that we called Essengeldturnschuhe (lunch money shoes) because they cost the same as the bi-weekly lunch. Did I mention they were ugly? I had a pair myself, and the only thing that saved me from embarrassment was the fact that most people wore them as well.

Lunch was always great and truly home-style. The lunch ladies were good chefs and really nice so long as you were nice to them. They made the same food you'd eat at home on weekends. We ate a variety of hot meals: stews, pork with veggies and potatoes, rice covered in a chicken-vegetable sauce, and even potato dumplings. I loved it when they made "dead grandma." It is a dish made of creamed blood sausage with potatoes and sauerkraut. Creepy, but delicious, even when it doesn't look very appetizing on the plate. I pretty much ate my lunch every single time and was rarely disappointed.

I can't tell you how many times my friends and I would race to the lunch room in the basement of one of the schools. When they served steamed dumplings, it was a given that we would go back into the line after we devoured our first round. We were only given two or three dumplings, but loved it when the lunch ladies could spare some extra ones. There were two kinds: one was a potato dumpling we would eat with red cabbage and pork. Another one was a white yeast dumpling served with a fruit sauce (usually in the summer, because it was not such a heavy dish). Those were great and almost like a bread roll only more doughy and warm. If the ladies would offer you two or three you would snatch them out of their hands before they could change their minds. I'm getting hungry just thinking about it. We never had peanut butter. We had never heard of it and didn't even know there was such a thing. There were no grilled cheese sandwiches or pizza. It was a real lunch, the kind you would get in a restaurant. You might think we were spoiled, but it was just healthy homemade food from scratch. Also, lunch was served on actual china plates and with real utensils. When you were done with your food, you had to go to the "check-out" station. There was a huge metal pot sitting on a chair next to a low table. That's where you had to scrape all your leftovers and then you had to separate your utensils from your dishes and put them on the table next to the scraps-pot accordingly. I can't think of a time, that I did not enjoy the lunch in school. There never was a dessert or a beverage with our lunches, but that wasn't unusual.

Field Trips

We had nice field trips that sometimes lasted as long as four days. We would go to the zoo or to some historic site. One time we went on a train ride to a camp in the middle of nowhere. Apparently, the teachers were not allowed to take us too far from home due to some sort of safety regulation. We had to hike with our backpacks through the forest and finally arrived at a tiny camp with small lodges around us. There were about six bunk beds in each lodge, with outdoor sinks and bathrooms. I liked to sleep on top every time, but scared everyone in the room when I fell out of it in the middle of the night. Ouch! We would hike through the forest for the next four days. It was fun, but creepy at the same time. I don't remember too much of it, but what I do remember are the wild boars we encountered on our hike back to the train station. We certainly could not complain about any dull moments.

On a different occasion, we had to bike to our destination. The town was about eight kilometers away at a lake. That was no big deal, but it was awful when you had to go slower than what you are used to. That camp had several small bungalows and a big house with several rooms and bunk beds. We stayed all the way on the top level overlooking the entrance of the property. It was pretty cool. The lake was in the back of the house, and we would have cookouts on the back patio. One time it was raining, but only half of the lake got rained on while we watched with amazement from the dry side. As you can tell, weather phenomena had not been among my special interests and I had no clue about what I was witnessing.

We would go swimming and kayaking there. One evening we had a disco in the main room of the house. We were dancing like crazy and thought we were just too cool!

One time, I had the opportunity to go on a field trip with my brother's class. I was very excited, because we were going to the Berlin Zoo. I loved animals and I couldn't wait to explore the wildlife and exhibits. After we visited some of the outdoor habitats, we went inside the reptile and amphibian house. Even though I generally liked frogs and turtle, I absolutely despised snakes. I always made sure to stay close to the group, but for some reason, I was drawn to the snakes. After a while, I realized that there were different people around me and started looking for the familiar faces of my brother's class. I searched the reptile house, but couldn't find any of them. Then I ran outside to look, but again I did not see the group anywhere. That's when I realized that I was lost. At first, I was mad that they left me behind. Then I was furious, because I recognized my own shortcomings of not having paid attention.

I started to wander away from the reptile exhibit in hopes I would catch up with the class very soon. Unfortunately, I never caught up to anyone and decided that the exit area of the zoo was the best location for me to be found. It seemed like I waited forever and I soon became restless. The ticket lady started giving me concerned looks and I was worried that she would report me to the authorities. For some reason, I was more afraid of that than being separated from the class. At that moment, I decided to exit the zoo and sit on a bench by the front gate.

Again, I waited without any success of being found. Luckily, I had some pocket money and started approaching the booth to purchase a new entry ticket. I was not sure how much time had actually passed during this entire ordeal, but it started to worry me. I thought, the best place to position myself was the reptile house. This time, I did not go inside again, but rather stayed right by the entrance door. After a short while, I heard my name being called and I was thrilled to see Thomas, a boy from my brother's class. He took my hand and guided me to the café area where everyone had gathered while a few kids were scouting for me. I received a very warm welcome and a big bowl of ice cream. This field trip was certainly unforgettable. I disliked snakes even more after that day.

Contests & Competitions

Remember a time as a child when you wanted to win a big prize or trophy? Yes, me too. I was in fifth grade when the announcement was made to create something that would make a difference in your life or the lives of your friends.

You had to build a model with a material of your choice. You had to design it, create it, and then present it. I partnered up with a friend of mine in hopes of making it easier. We were going to create a grand playground. We did not have a playground in the entire town, not even on the school grounds, not even a swing. Outside recess meant standing in little groups talking or playing a jumping game with really long rubber strings. We decided to come up with a model that displayed what our playground should look like. Our material was wood. We sketched the design out on paper and made adjustments all over the place. We had a certain size platform to fit everything on, so we needed to be sure not to overcrowd anything. We decided on a seesaw, a swing, a carousel with horse carriages, and some climbing equipment. We had it all figured out in our heads. It was perfect. As we started on our grand project, tracing our designs on pieces of wood and attempting to cut them out with hand saws, we realized it was not quite as easy as we had thought. My friend soon became frustrated and left me hanging. I certainly was not going to give up. I wanted to win, even though I had no clue what the prize actually was. I went home and complained to my dad, the handy man. I showed him my ideas on paper and told him how I wanted it to all go together and have actual moving pieces. I don't know what he was thinking, but he did agree to help me. We made alterations along the way and cut a couple things from the project to make the pieces bigger so we could actually make them movable. It seemed to take forever, months, but it was really only a week or so. Then, the fun part began: time to decorate and paint the model playground. I was very detail oriented and did not want to mess it up. The entire wooden playground project ended up looking fantastic with all the colorful paint and movable parts. The only downside was that it was heavy!!! Pride kept me from asking for help carrying that thing to school. I started to worry after I had submitted my project, comparing it to all the others in the hallway. At the end of the day, I was quite convinced I would never be able to win anything. I thought mine looked great, but I wasn't sure exactly what the judges were looking for. I hated that uncertainty. At the end of the week, we had the big announcement of the winners. We had to assemble in the schoolyard arranged in classes and wearing our uniforms. I was so busy wallowing in the misery of failure that I almost missed the announcement of my name! Not only did I win, but I won first place!!! There were no fancy prizes, no gift certificate or money or movie tickets. I won a bar of chocolate, colored pencils, paint, a block of white paper and markers. I was so proud; I might have glowed in the dark! The shortest person in the school stood very tall that day. I did thank my dad and probably shared my chocolate with him, but the craft supplies were all mine.

We also had the occasional sports competition. I still have pins from that time. Usually, it was an all-day event on a Saturday. It was held at a bigger sports complex with a big outdoor track. There were different schools competing and we were divided by school, age and classrooms. I was usually chosen to run the 100m track and the 400m run. Hurdles and long jumps were not really my favorite, but teachers really appreciated my speed on the track. Most of my friends and school mates hated sports day, but I secretly loved it. I suppose you can say that I was very competitive and loved every chance I got to prove to myself that I was the fastest runner.

Additionally, I enjoyed being part of a team and something greater than myself.

Summer

We had summer vacation for about six weeks each year. It always seemed to end on or right after my birthday. Our summers were great. The temperatures were just right and it was never too hot or humid. My parents always worked when we had school vacations. Some of my friends' moms were home for reasons unknown to me; so they kept an eye on us. When my family moved into the country and into our own house in 1986, our summer routine changed as well. I was a bit older, and I had more liberties. I made lots of friends at the new school in town and always hung out with them. Our favorite summer pastime was to go swimming. The lake of choice, the only lake nearby, was about eight kilometers (about five miles) away. As you can imagine, this was more like a day trip. We habitually had a time set when we would meet up. That generally provided me ample time to get my drink bottle and fill it up with anything I could find, usually water, although sometimes we had raspberry syrup in the house and I could mix it in. I made sandwiches (salami was always my favorite) and maybe threw in some butter cookies and an apple. This would be my food stash for the day. I'd always bring one or two Marks with me, just in case we might decide to walk another two kilometers (just over a mile) into the next town to shop for snacks at the little "mom and pop" store.

So, we all had our bicycles ready and off we went. It was always fun to ride, and we did follow all road rules. Of course, the lack of traffic was helpful. You could ride the entire way to the lake and not encounter a single car. We spent all day at the lake and generally didn't get home until 6 or 7.p.m. We were lucky our parents trusted us so much.

When we got tired of our juice mixes and sandwiches, we would take walks through the forest around the lake and usually made a pit stop in the nearby corn field. Now, we never ate corn as an actual side dish at home. We didn't know about corn on the cob smothered in butter. Corn was considered animal food. One time we just tried it out of curiosity. We picked it off the corn stalk and peeled it. It was very starchy and a bit sweet as well. It was really not too bad. Still, we never told our parents about it, because we basically took the corn without asking and we weren't supposed to eat cattle feed.

Once in a while, we decided to take the long walk into the next town. The store that was our customary destination was located at the far end of town; not very convenient for anyone coming from our direction. Anyway, we would walk in our bare feet all the way to that store just to buy cookies and club cola. I was never a big fan of sodas, but liked to treat myself to club cola. If you've never had it, but you like Coca-Cola, you should try it. I always bought the round butter cookies. The lady in the store always gave us a strange look. We must have looked like poor little kids wearing only our bathing suits and no shoes. I wonder if "no shirt, no shoes, no service" was invented because of people like us? Just kidding.

Of course, the big bummer had to be the walk all the way back. It was quite a workout, although we made up the burned calories by eating and drinking our snacks. It was always worth the trip.

I biked to the lake every single day, sometimes in my bare feet. One of my friends lived really close to the lake, and I spent the night there many times. That was my shortcut to the nice, refreshing water. There was a big jumping tower at the lake. We attempted various jumping styles in an effort to produce the biggest splash. Unfortunately, the best maneuver was also the most painful: jumping at a very strange angle so that you would just barely miss a flat back flop. I had never seen my backside in that particular shade of red before. I was the talk of the party that day, and my performance was never reenacted or reproduced the same way. Oh, yeah, - I had style! Freestyle, that is.

Because it was a lake, we encountered all sorts of lake creatures. Once a snake swam by in front of my face, and that was the last time I opened my eyes under the water there. I jumped quite high, maybe even set a new record. I'll never know. I was also stabbed and sliced wounds by crawfish. It's too bad I didn't know you could eat them. It was painful and quite bloody without even a tasty meal to show for it. At least showing off my battle wounds made it all worthwhile.

Twice in my life, I went to the Ferienlager (summer camp). I was not exactly a big fan of the idea at first, but I always enjoyed it once I got there. I was eight years old when my parents sent me to camp for the first time. I don't remember where we went, but I think it was near Koenigswusterhausen. My brother went as well. Even though we didn't exactly like each other at the time, we sat next to each other on the bus. It sure made me feel better. Once we arrived, we were split into age groups and my brother had to go to the other end of the camp site. I was in a group of about ten girls. We had a room on the second floor in a big building full of bunk beds. I chose the top of the one nearest the door. Our camp leader was a girl. I don't remember her name, but she was nice. We always had to get up early and walk to the cafeteria. We had the day all laid out for us with tons of activities. Besides certain group activities, we were able to choose two classes for the two weeks we were there. During my first week, I learned how to make apple turnovers in the baking class. I was really good at it and could not wait to get home to show my parents my new baking talent. I did show them, so much so that I think they couldn't stand the sight of a turnover for a long time. In my mind, I was now a baking pro.

The second week I dedicated to my dad. I took a criminal justice class. It was so much fun. We were looking for clues all over the camp site. We were provided with that gray powder to discover fingerprints and find matching people. We found footprints in the dirt that we filled with white plaster to preserve the print for further investigation. The last major project of the class was to find a stolen bicycle. I had a blast and felt like a real police officer. We found the bike after a few hours. We had to use all of our acquired investigator skills, and it was totally awesome!

One other event took place in that particular camp, and I have very mixed feelings about it. Ever since the second day at camp, people had been talking about Neptunfest (King Neptune). We were told by the camp leaders that only the bad kids would be chosen and given to King Neptune. Now, I was not a bad kid, but for some reason, I didn't buy the whole story. On the day of the Neptunfest, it was all fun and games first. We made all kinds of crafts related to the water. Then we watched the ceremony of King Neptune coming on the boat to the campsite. He looked scary to me. Then they started to announce names of kids. Each time a child's name got called, you could see the "terror" in their eyes. They got up and started running away, only to be caught right away by Neptune's helpers. Then they would be baptized and thrown into the water. They called *my* name. Oh yeah. My heart might have skipped a couple beats, but I totally gave them a run for their money. I ran through the whole crowd of people, jumped over planks, through the forest and all over the beach. They were totally exhausted by the time they finally caught me. It was about six people in the end who were chasing me. Then I had to stand in front of King Neptune. He said all kinds of things to me and then baptized me by pouring the icky white gunk all over my long hair and then they threw me into the lake. Once I got out, they presented me with my certificate that had my new "Sea name" on it. Apparently, King Neptune had chosen it for me, because it fit my personality. It was fun, but getting that gummy stuff out of my hair was a real pain. I think it took me several days to get the last of it out. After that, I was the talk of my side of camp, because I had been a fugitive for so long. Those were my 15 minutes of fame, I guess. My brother of all people was actually really nice to me. I only saw him once in camp, but he did talk to me and asked how I was doing. Prior to that day, I had come back to my room, lay down and hurt my head on my pillow. He had put two bottles of club cola under it. I was totally happy and proud to have a cool brother like that.

Two weeks went by really quickly and the bus ride home was sad. I missed my new friends and made sure we had exchanged addresses to write letters.

The following year, when I was nine years old, I went to another two week camp at the Baltic Sea. I think people told me at the time that the water was salty, but of course, I didn't remember that part until I jumped into it and splashed it all around. We had some kind of contest at the beach which included throwing a firefighter's boot as far as we could. It didn't seem difficult until I tried it, being only four feet tall and at least twelve inches deep in the sand. The whole endeavor was very awkward, and then the sand got in my eyes. Whoever came up with that idea obviously was not my size. I should have been given a small garden gnome boot.

Anyway, the mornings were torturous. We had to do exercises for at least fifteen to thirty minutes. It wasn't as though we couldn't do it, but we had just been woken up by the same song that blared out of the camp speakers at us every morning. You had to be deaf not to hear it. "Guten Morgen, liebe Sorgen seid ihr auch schon alle da?" Nothing quite like it anywhere else. It got in your head and stayed there until the next morning. I still know the lyrics!

We did lots of crafts and I learned how to make braids. That was a painful task at first because I couldn't get the hang of it right away. After plenty of practice, I was finally able to make my skirt out of some sort of green material. Just in time for the party!

There were also surprise night walks. I could almost sense when that particular night was coming up or was right around the corner. People started speculating about when it would happen. We even started to sleep with our day clothes on. One night, when thankfully I was already dressed and ready, our group leader just bust in, flicked the lights on and said, "It's time. Ready? Let's go!" Then they shoved a flashlight into my hand and off we went, into the woods without any idea where to go or how long we'd be stuck out there. Thankfully my dad had indirectly prepared me for those sorts of things by taking me on his nocturnal hunting trips for wild boar and deer. He didn't realize it at the time, of course. I was doing fine during the night walk and those "wild" noises of owls and crickets didn't scare me. I did, however, encounter Glühwürmchen (glow worms) for the first time. They glow, but they don't fly. They just sit there in the grass, glowing.

The best thing about those night walks was the huge bonfire waiting at the end. We roasted potatoes and dough on a sick. So much fun! We didn't have any marshmallows, and none of us had even heard of s'mores. Sweet dough on a stick is much tastier anyway, and more rugged!

Chores

Chores started at a young age. I like to think this was our parents' way to teach us self-reliance and independence. It worked for me. Looking back, I am very thankful for it.

When we were living in an apartment, the chores were quite different from the ones we had after we moved into our house in the countryside. My brother and I were taught to divide and conquer our chores. Besides regular daily chores like making our beds, and cleaning our room, we shared and putting our shoes, jackets, and other accessories where they were supposed to go, and we always had Saturday chores. Those were the big ones. They included vacuuming, sweeping the stairway of our apartment level and washing the steps as well. This meant carrying a big bucket of water from step to step without making a big watery mess. Also, my mom only cooked hot meals on the weekend. This meant washing the dishes after meals became a chore for the children. My brother and I always took turns with who washed and who dried and put the dishes away. It might sound straightforward, but my mom was very particular about her dishes. Of course, there were plenty of other chores, especially after we moved.

Our Move to the Countryside

In 1986, we moved to a house in a country. I recall touring the house once before my parents purchased it. It was occupied by a family with two boys. The wallpaper was an ugly brown and I found the house to be claustrophobic. It was quite remote, situated about 800m away from the main road. Beside the neighbors directly across from them, the house was almost the last one on the street. There was one little black house a bit further down. It was occupied by Olga, the "witch."

The house we purchased was quite large with a nice yard. However, the former owners did not take good care of the house or the property. The upstairs was occupied by an old couple in their late 70s. They were quite odd. The old man was very tall, maybe seven feet, and made very loud noises when he was walking around. The woman always carried some metal bucket with mysterious contents. Every time she walked down the steps, I was afraid she would rip out the railing, because she seemed to depend almost entirely on that for support. Then she would walk out the backyard and use the outhouse, which seemed both strange and disgusting. There was a bathroom upstairs, after all.

When my dad finally walked upstairs to collect their rent, he encountered all sorts of physical obstacles. That was the day we found out that they were hoarders. According to my dad, they had boxes, furniture pieces and everything else they owned and collected piled to the ceiling, leaving only enough room for a narrow pathway. That was really freaking me out. My parents did their best to have them clean out the rooms, and also forbade the man to go down to the basement. He was in very bad health and my parents did not want him to fall on the steep basement steps. The man never listened. One day my parents came home and found him dead in the basement. Apparently, he had decided to go down there and add more coal to the fire but fell and hit his head. His wife never heard him. I cannot tell you how glad I was that I wasn't the one who had discovered him, although I easily could have been.

I say that, because, when I came home from school, my brother's job was to add one bucket of coal and cokes into the oven. Since he usually had a string of excuses not to do it, it soon became my job.

After the incident and death of the man, his wife still lived upstairs, but had more visitors. Usually her daughter came to check on her, and eventually they decided to move her in with them.

When we moved in, there was so much to do besides the general unpacking. The basement had four rooms; one being the "heater room." In this particular room was the iron oven that heated the entire house. There was also a side room where the coal and coke was kept, along with two wicker baskets filled with chopped wood. We could not open the other rooms without having the precarious content fall all over us. As you can imagine, the clearing of those rooms took quite some time.

Another major hiccup was finding out that the basement would flood after heavy rain. This happened a couple times after we moved in. It was not your usual wet basement; it would flood with nearly a foot of standing water after the rainfalls. Since the house was not designed to naturally drain the water, we had to manually drain the basement. I can assure you that it was one of the most painstaking jobs ever known.

Each of us took a bucket, filled it with the water in the basement, carried it up the steep steps and poured it out on the other side of the yard. It took hours to get the water out! In addition, it made the coal wet and we could only use what was on top, hoping the rest would dry out soon.

Because the house was heated by coal and cokes, we had to put in our annual delivery order. Every summer season we received about a ton of coal and coke which was usually dropped off right outside the bathroom window; between the house and the garage. Of course, we had to shovel the entire load by hand into the basement through a 30x30cm window! Strangely, my dad and my brother never seemed to be around when this particular delivery came. How convenient for them. It took my mom and me hours to clear the spot and get everything into the basement. First, we would fill metal buckets with the coal and cokes and then carry one by one into the basement. Once we somewhat cleared the area enough to make out the window to the basement, I would go inside and open the window to make the coal fall into the basement room where we kept it. My mom would shovel from the outside and I would help from inside. We would take turns and adjust our positions based on the progress we were making. At the end of it all we were totally covered in black dust and hardly recognizable.

In order to keep the house warm, my mom would get up very early in the morning to put coal into the basement oven. By the time my brother and I would get up, the water was warm and the rooms were cozy. It was my brother's responsibility to add more coal to the furnace when he came home from school, but he often forgot. In order to keep him out of trouble, I would usually go down the basement, scrape all the ashes out, add cokes, stir the embers and add a new bucket of coal. I would check on it often to ensure the fire was still going. I was only eight years old then, but as I mentioned before, we were raised to be self-reliant. I mostly did it, because I didn't have a choice.

Another big project we dealt with after moving into the house was the backyard. It had such tall weeds that you couldn't even see the walking path or individual garden plots. It was quite a lot of work to cut them down and do some landscaping. There were several fruit trees in the yard, a long walkway to the outhouse at the back of the property used by the upstairs tenants, and a big old shed. We also found a well with a functioning water pump. After several weeks, the backyard was finally recognizable as such, and we could start to landscape and plant seeds for fruit and vegetables.

The beautiful thing about living in the country was that we also had all sorts of animals. We always had a dog. Once a year, our dog had puppies. You just can't beat playing with six or more cute little dachshunds every single day. They were adorable. I was always upset when people came by to look at them and then eventually bought them one by one.

We also had nine rabbits, twenty ducks, and ten geese, tons of chickens, pigeons, and pigs. It was like living on a farm. Thankfully, no cows or horses!! As you can imagine, taking care of all those animals was a lot of work and took some time. Every day after school, I was to feed to chickens. We had a huge metal container in the garage that held all the chicken feed. I had to add a certain amount in a red bucket and then carry it into the backyard to feed the chickens. I swear they could tell by the color of the bucket that they were about to get food. As soon as I started walking out of the garage, they went crazy; flying around and bumping into each other. It was bizarre. It eventually got so bad that I couldn't even open the gate to get into their fenced area. I had to throw a handful of feed across the fence to have them run away from the gate so I could then finally enter and put the feed into the appropriate containers for them. I didn't like the chickens. I found them annoying, but they were good eats.

I enjoyed feeding the rabbits much more. They were cute, soft, more laid back and friendly. When autumn came, I had to keep reminding myself not to get too attached to them, though. After all, they were food, not pets. Of course, this was the case for all our animals, because it was economically smart. Raising your own animals for food and growing your own vegetables and fruit was a big money saver. Furthermore, it gave you the opportunity to eat something you could not always buy in the store.

Speaking of fruits, we had apple trees, a plum tree, a pear tree and a tart cherry tree. We not only ate the fruit right off the trees, but also used those for canning, baking, making marmalade and, my dad's favorite, wine. I always seemed to be the one picking all the fruit for his wine, but I never got to drink it. I have to admit that it was a lot of fun learning the entire winemaking process and participating in all separate stages of making the wine. We never made our own labels or anything, but that didn't really matter at the time.

Do you know what else was great about creating our own food concoctions? We knew exactly what was in it, we could decide how sweet we wanted our jam to be, and eating food we knew we had grown ourselves was very rewarding. Nothing was more satisfying than seeing others of our family and friends enjoying the fruit of our labor.

We were also very handy people. My dad would usually work on some type of building project; from hunting stands to rabbit hutches and pigeon lofts. I was merely the apprentice, but certainly loved the hands-on learning experience. I tried to build my own bird houses or toy weapons, but that was about it. One thing I was really good at was making my own fishing poles. We had two big hazelnut bushes in the back corner of the yard. Besides eating the hazelnuts, I loved the flexibility of the branches. I decided that they would make fantastic poles for fishing. I would look for a tall, straight branch; not too thick and not too thin. I always had to keep in mind that I would have to transport the pole while riding my bike for several kilometers, keeping it at a perfect length to balance on my bike, long enough to classify it as a fishing pole and keep certain flexibility in the branch. After some trial and error, I got the hang of creating some great fishing poles.

Snow Days

First of all, I have to tell you that "snow days" did not exist in East Germany. Nobody cared if it snowed, when or how much, because we were expected to show up no matter what. There were no school busses waiting somewhere to pick you up, no school buses to be late or unable to maneuver the snowy and icy roads. It was all up to us!

So, we bundled up and went on our way to school or work. I just remember a lot of walking everywhere. This often included my hat blowing off my head, my scarf either choking me or not giving enough protection, or my gloves becoming completely soaked, because I couldn't help making snowballs and throwing them at my brother. Retaliation was bitter. Have you ever had snow shoved down the back of your shirt or your face iced over? Then you know what I am talking about. Ouch!

Winter and snow were objects of both love and hate for me. I always wanted to love it, but I just couldn't stay warm. As soon as my fingers or toes got cold, it was all over. I was envious, watching everyone else play for hours while I gave myself an internal high-five for lasting thirty minutes outside. I started having little contests with myself to beat my own times every time I went outside to battle the cold. It was becoming ridiculous! My dad always told me that I never dressed warm enough and that it was part of my problem. I disagreed, of course. As a result, I was the shortest kid in the entire town who had to wear her dad's gloves, hat and scarf. Picture that! I also had a "little" problem giving up on things. So, not only did I try to beat my own time scores, but I "had" to carry my own snow and ski equipment down three stories all by myself. I was offered help several times, but that Napoleon complex always had the last word, with mixed results. Sometimes it was great, but most of the time I ended up rolling or falling down concrete steps getting all tangled up in my skis, sled or whatever I was carrying. Despite all that, I never admitted that I was wrong. It was always some type of unforeseen obstacle, such as shoes on the stairs, or flower pots that kept me from safely reaching my goals.

I believe I was about five or six years old when from somewhere appeared those really awesome blue and white skis. Oh, I was beyond excited. After "rolling" down the concrete steps again, I buckled my boots in and off I went. Nobody had shown me how to ski. After falling and getting back up countless times, I actually had a couple of great runs. It was only on the flat of the road, but it worked for me. Skiing was my new gig. Every day I was on a mission to be faster and better. It's hard to believe that it snowed so much then. You never doubted or wondered whether it would snow. It just happened, because the calendar said it was winter.

After we had moved into the suburbs, my brother and I decided to build an igloo in the backyard. I think we uncovered the entire yard to make those snowy building blocks and seemed to have brought spring back all around us. It was a lot of work, and we were dripping with sweat. At least I wasn't cold! After hours and hours of making snow blocks to build this thing, we ended up with a construction that did not mirror at all the image we made out in our heads. The igloo was not really round, but more like an oval. There were lots of gaps in the roof. In a real survival situation, we would have been in trouble. Fortunately for us, the front door was only fifty meters away. The best part was climbing inside and proudly pointing out all the great work we put into it. Let me tell you, it was a true team effort. My brother and I were not especially close, but there were times in our childhood where we came together and created great things. This was one of those great times. We were talking about it for days, checking it out from the kitchen window and making plans for improvements, going back outside for closer inspections and again pointing out areas that needed to be fixed. It lasted about one week, and then the igloo slowly started to flatten and eventually was unrecognizable. But the story survived.

Vacation

Our family did not really go on vacation. Our "adventures" were day trips. Usually, my parents would wake my brother and me very early in the morning. I never had a clue where we were going, but I always did love surprises.

One time we went to the Karl-May-Museum in Radebeul, near Dresden. I was ecstatic! You have to know by now that I had a slight obsession with Native Americans from an early age. I have no idea why. Maybe it was, because they were so different from me; in looks and lifestyle. All I ever wanted as a child was to live in a tepee; a big one with a fire inside. I never liked horses though, so, I'm assuming I never imagined myself riding one on the Plaines.

Whatever the reason, the museum was a dream comes true for me. I immersed myself in all the exhibitions and took in every bit of visual information I possibly could. The costumes were always my favorite part; with the feathers and the "peace pipe." I never liked smoking or people smoking around me, but this particular one was for peace talks, after all, so you had to have one of those pipes. I'm pretty sure my brother became bored early on, but I probably wished I could move into the museum and just hang out.

I guess the main reason I caught an interest in the Native American culture was due to stories by Karl May. He was an author who wrote many stories from his adventures in the later 1800s. One of my favorite characters he created was Old Shatterhand. I didn't read the stories when I was really little, but I loved the movies that were based on them. I still have the theme music on vinyl record.

Our only big family vacation was going to Brotterode in the Thuringian Forest. It was a winter vacation and we traveled by train. All I can remember is a lot of snow, whiteouts from winter storms and plows pushing the snow so high it touched the second story window of the houses in town. Our vacation was two weeks long and a lot of fun.

We stayed in a small apartment with only one room that was divided by a mid-sized wall made of furniture. My brother and I were sleeping in a bunk bed and my parents on a fold-out couch. It was a tiny room, but nobody was complaining.

Well, my dad must not have liked it, because I remember his slipper flying across the room and hitting me in the head while I was talking to my brother and, apparently, being too loud. I remember being so startled that I didn't know whether to be scared or to laugh. I had no intention of immediately handing the slipper over, but rather quietly placed it next to the other one the next morning.

First of all, I did not like cold weather very much. Secondly, the snow was very deep and, as a short person stuck in a mustard-colored snowsuit, it was not exactly convenient to walk through all that white fluff. I found myself being carried on my dad's shoulders the majority of the time. Don't judge me; I was only three years old. My dad gifted me a yellow-brown hat and I loved it. It was the only hat I would wear, which upset my mom at times because she had made me so many hats prior to that. Maybe it was because it matched my snowsuit. Since my dad carried me everywhere, my hat often got stuck in tree branches during our hikes. We were pretty much hiking and sledding the entire time we were there. I am not sure if there was a television in the room because I don't recall watching any TV. We did play a lot of board games. We are all very competitive and even my parents would not let any of us kids win just to make us feel better. I especially remember playing the game "Sorry" and how many times my pieces got knocked out of the game. We also played card games, and my favorite one was "Rummy." As you can tell, there was a lot of family bonding going on.

Television/Radio

Radio was our biggest entertainment. It was a staple of our morning routine, after work, and on the weekends. Either while we were eating breakfast, getting ready for school, or as an entertaining background during coffee breaks and while working on projects, inside or outside the house, the radio was usually on. My parents had a favorite station (Spree Radio?) and we listened to it all the time. Especially on the weekends, I remember hearing the program "Spree Athen." I was introduced to music this way and soon had my favorite artists picked out. I would listen to their songs on the vinyl records and made certain I would not miss them on the music show "Bong" on the television. If I was not in the room when the Pop charts show was airing, my mom would always call me, especially when my favorite artists performed. It was hilarious, the way I was definitely crushing on a couple of them early on.

I was also slightly obsessed with listening to stories on my record player – over and over and over again. I had a few favorites and probably drove my brother crazy. We did not have headphones then. It certainly didn't bother me and, apparently, I was blind to eye-rolling from anyone.

The TV was not usually turned on until the very end of the day. During school vacations, we always enjoyed the kids' movies that aired starting at 11a.m., but in general our television was underutilized. I'm not complaining, especially considering I was often turned into the "walking remote control." We only had one or two channels, but I still had to get up to change them and to control the volume. I guess that was one way to get your exercise in.

I loved all the shows they had for kids. They always transported me into a different world; and I wished I could somehow be part of it. We had several Russian and Czechoslovakian shows that I liked. One of my favorite shows was the "Rabbit and the Wolf." It was a Russian cartoon, and I guess you can say it was the equivalent of "Tom and Jerry".

The fairy tale movies were always amazing, especially the ones with the witch that lived in the woods, in a house that had chicken feet and could walk and turn around by itself – the witch Baba Jaga. It certainly taught us to pay more attention while out playing in the woods, as well as to stay away from the red mushrooms with white dots on them.

Then I discovered a show that had nothing to do with entertainment at all. It was an exercise program, and I loved it! At the early age of five years old, I was engulfed in the program "Medizin nach Noten" (Google translate: "Medicine to notes"). It was about ten minutes long. I saw a person on an elevated platform demonstrating aerobic moves, and then there were about eighty people in front of the stage moving along with the person. There was some pop music playing to make it more fun and exciting, I guess. So, there I was, in the living room in front of the television moving along with everyone else. To quench my thirst, I had my chocolate milk handy at all times. I didn't count calories or anything; to me, it was just fun, and I made sure to catch the episodes as often as possible. We even owned a vinyl record at some point that had the music on it and the exercise moves were printed on the sleeve. I utilized this occasionally but preferred the program on the television which allowed me to see the movements. Nobody ever did this program with me. I have no idea how I discovered it, but apparently, that's where my love for structured fitness began.

We also had a TV program for children in the evening, "Das Sandmaennchen" (The sandman). It was a great show, and was aired around the time you were about to be sent to bed. He was always going on some type of adventure, into space, the dessert, a hot-air balloon; honestly, he had the "coolest" gadgets and means of transportation. He would show us a short story with some of my favorite characters: Pittiplatsch (a kobold), Schnatterienchen (a duck), Moppi (a dog), Frau Elster (a magpie), Herr Fuchs (a fox) and Plumps (a water goblin with purple hair). I loved all of them. I even listened to the character's adventures on vinyl over and over again. They had the perfect sense of humor and always had a great storyline and great takeaways to be learned.

A Moment in Time (or History for the Rest of the World)

So, apparently, I lived some sort of "prison" life in East Germany. At least that's what a lot of people think when the term "East Germany" comes up. Now, I want you to know that I am not exactly disagreeing, but I was a child during that time and I am writing this story from that point of view. I never asked my parents what they were thinking, at least not at that time.

I did not grow up in the city of Berlin, but rather twenty-four miles away. That may not seem very far away, but in that world it was. What I mean is that I did not see the Berlin Wall every day. It was not in my face on a daily basis as a reminder that there was something on the other side. I lived in the suburbs, the country, in a small town of 2500 people. My mom took me to Berlin either once in a blue moon for fun or to take me to my cardiology appointments. I loved Berlin. I loved going on the city train and to the Kaufhaus. I loved the "feel" of the city and the hidden excitement that whirled around. I think I might have skipped my way through the city more than walking. It never occurred to me as a child that the country, and the city, was divided. We had to get off at the "last" station (Friedrichstrasse). I remember that it was announced on the overhead speakers at the station that you needed to "get off. This is the last station." I remember seeing the train tracks going far beyond the last station, but didn't know why we absolutely had to get off. Honestly, I didn't really care. All I wanted to do was see the Neptune Fountain, the World Clock, the TV tower, and get my "special" milk (H-Milch) from the grocery store on the bottom floor of the Kaufhaus. I always thought of them as "fancy", because they didn't come in the usual glass bottles. They had two types which I loved! One came in a small Tetra pack the same size as today's juice boxes. It had a slight coffee flavor to it. Another one I really liked was in the shape of a pyramid. It came in white milk (blue and white) or chocolate (brown and white). I never saw it in any store, except in Berlin. So, yes, maybe I loved Berlin, because of the milk. They also had Currywurst! Oh, and in this one ice creams store, they had a waffle that looked like a clam shell to put your ice cream into – I thought it was amazing!

One time, when I was five years old, my mom took me to the top of the Fernsehturm (Television tower). It was built in the 60s and is 368m tall. To this day, it remains the only city TV tower in Europe and is the tallest building in the city of Berlin. All I remember from that time is how small everything was. I thought I could see into infinity. It was a moment in my life that I will never forget. It blew my mind how tiny the buses, cars, and people were down below. The feeling of being so high up and looking through those large windows to see the entire city was mesmerizing. I do not remember seeing the Brandenburg Gate or the Siegessaeule. I don't know why. I probably just didn't pay attention. I was only five years old and certainly didn't know what to look for. My parents didn't talk about "the other side" to avoid sparking any curiosity about it.

A couple years later, I remember going to Berlin to step inside the West German shop, otherwise known as the "Intershop." That was exciting. My dad's great aunt moved to West Berlin (Spandau) after her husband passed away. I don't know how that was possible, but it happened. She would come visit us once a year or so. It was always a surprise. Besides bringing us sweets like Haribo bears and chocolate, she gave us West German money. Not much, just five Marks or so. Obviously, I couldn't spend it anywhere in East Germany, except for that one store in Berlin, Intershop, where we could go to and buy something with our West German Marks! It felt almost uncomfortable going inside. It was really dark with some weird ultraviolet blue lighting. I remember two ladies staring at us when we entered. It was just weird and I felt totally out of place. They had all kinds of items for sale – chocolates, candy, alcohol, toys, soaps, etc. Nothing I had ever seen before. It was surreal, like entering an entirely different world. I don't really remember what my brother bought or if my mom got anything, but they had chocolate, and I loved chocolate. We bought some and walked out. I almost felt like I had done something wrong just by having it. It's not as though I had stolen it, but I felt like everyone who looked at me knew where I had been. I could not wait to get away from that place.

In 1984, thanks to my mom's workplace, I was able to go and see a Christmas/Winter Play in the Palast der Republik. The Palace of the

Republic in Berlin was the seat of the parliament of the German Democratic Republic. There were also two large auditoria, art galleries, a theater, thirteen restaurants, a bowling alley, a post office, and a discothèque inside. I remember enjoying the play, but the fact that I was able to see the grand interior of the palace was breathtaking. I felt like I was part of the greatest movie ever made. It blew my mind that people went in and out of that place on a daily basis and maybe never felt as excited as I did. At the age of six, I had never seen that many chandeliers, lights, glass, and mirrors in one place. It was definitely, one of the fanciest and grandest places I had ever been. I was never the princess type and was not easily impressed, but that place looked nothing like I expected after merely seeing the rather drab exterior.

In 1988 or thereabouts, my mom had to go to the Charite' in Berlin. It was a hospital full of specialists. She had a ruptured eardrum that needed surgical repair. She was in the room towards the top of the building and facing the West. Due to the close proximity of West Berlin, and the fact that the radio waves and TV channels were easily transmitted to "our" side, my mom had to sign a paper promising she would not watch any West German Television. My dad and I went to visit her. She shared a room with another woman, so we walked to the very end of the hallway right by the big windows.

There it was, a view I would never forget. It was almost surreal, and I remember questioning what I saw. It was the Death Zone! It sent a shiver down my spine, because it reminded me of what a warzone must look like. For the first time in my life, I saw the Berlin Wall in all its glory: the barbed wire, the soldiers with rifles, the dogs, the watchtower, the open space and the other side with a wall. 167 kilometers of separation of East and West Berlin. I felt dislocated and all of a sudden, the world turned gray in front of me. It was like a real-life history movie, only I was actively participating; as an observer. I saw so many cars and big pictures on stands, which I later learned were billboards. "*I have never seen those cars before,*" I thought. "*What are those pictures?*" and "*What am I looking at?*" I asked my mom if we could talk about that and if we could go over there sometime. She said, "No. We will go to prison if we cross that wall." I said that was stupid. There you have it. A moment in time. I thought about that a lot on my way home and long after, but I never asked my parents any more questions about it. It was the first time that I truly realized that there was a division in the country. I wanted to know more, but it wasn't as though I could "Google it" or go to the library and read all about it. I am certain any information about the West I would have had access to, had been manipulated in a way that made them look bad, just like the West had preconceived ideas about us in the East. I was always aware of the last stations for trains and all, but I had never had such a visual experience before. You might call me naïve, but when you don't have a dividing wall in front of you every day, you tend to not question anything, because you don't know it exists. It was quite strange from that point on, for me at least.

The Day Everything Changed

It was a typical Saturday morning in October of 1989. My brother and I were going to school until lunch time. As usual, we rode our bikes. We were never late or very early arriving at school, but that day something was "off." The usual bike traffic was missing and hardly any bikes were parked by the school that morning. Not thinking much about it, we went our separate ways to our classrooms. Mine was all the way on the other side of the building in the very back corner. My brother's was on the second floor.

It didn't take long for us to find out something was truly not right. Nobody was in my class. I walked out of the classroom into the hallway and went across the corridor to check the other rooms. Besides a few students here and there, nobody was around. The few students attending class that day walked out into the hallways looking confused and were just trying to make sense of it all. Something happened. The teachers who were present decided to send us home.

As you can imagine, the ride back to our house was a mix of happiness and bewilderment. When we arrived home, my mom was starting to cook lunch. She was surprised to see us home already and we explained the entire experience to her. The borders to West Berlin and West Germany had been opened. Everyone went to Berlin to see it unfold and to participate in the historic moment called "The Fall of the Berlin Wall."

It was a very strange feeling, and I was not quite sure how to wrap my mind around it. Honestly, I did not even know what impact it had in my life; at that moment.

All I knew was that life as I knew it was about to change in a big way.

....

To be continued...

Some of my stamp collection:

My first, but unknown, exposure to Mickey
Mouse.

A lot of these stamps were taken from actual letters we received in the mail.

Stamp albums with a handwritten

sign stating "Bitte nicht stoeren"

(Please, do not disturb)

A German-Russian Dictionary that was handed

down to me from my Dad.

Besuch von einem Panda

This was one of the first books my mom bought from

the woman who owned the bookstore in town.

It was always one of my favorite ones and sparked

my interest in reading and other world cultures.

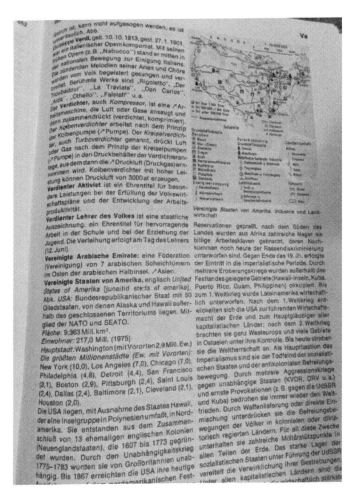

A snapshot out of the East German Encyclopedia of what

we were taught about the United States of America and

what it meant to be a Pionier (next picture).

bestehen und wächst ... Folgende Klassen wer-
... Algen-, Schlauch-
... Fruchtkörper vieler Stän-
... (z. B. Champignon), manche
... Geschmacks ungenießbar (z. B.
... giftig (z. B. Knollenblätter-
... sollte nur die Pilze neh-
... genau kennt. Pilzver-
... zum Tode führen. Abb.
... im Militärwesen sind für mili-
...aufgaben ausgebildete und
... der Landstreitkräfte. Sie
... mit der Truppe in Angriffs-
...handlungen. Ihre Aufgaben sind
... und Brückenbau und die Be-
... Hindernissen. Abb.

... bauen eine Pontonbrücke.

*Pionierorganisation, Abb. 2: Junger Pionier beim Gruß.
Holzschnitt von Gerd Thielemann.*

Rat der Freunde	Zentralrat der FDJ	
Rat der Freunde	Bezirksleitung der FDJ	Leitungsfunktionen üben Jugendliche und Erwachsene aus
Rat der Freunde	Kreisleitung der FDJ	
Freundschafts-pionierleiter	Freundschaftsrat	Pionier-freundschaft
Gruppen-pionierleiter	Gruppenrat	Pioniergruppe
	Brigadeleiter	Pionierbrigade

...organisation „Ernst Thälmann" wurde
... 1948 auf Beschluß des Zentralrates der
... Sie ist die einheitliche politische
...organisation der Kinder und wird von der
... Grundlage der Beschlüsse der SED
... Schüler bis zum 14. Lebensjahr
... der Pionierorganisation werden,
... das Statut anerkennt. Alle Jung- und
...pioniere einer Schule bilden die Pio-
...schaft. Sie gliedert sich in *Jung-Pionier-*
... (Klassen 1–3) und *Thälmann-Pionier-*
... (Klassen 4–7). In den Thälmann-Pionier-

*Pionierorganisation, Abb. 1: Aufbau der Pionierorgani-
sation „Ernst Thälmann".*

FDJ = Freihe Deutsche Jugend (Free German Youth)

patch.

My mom used to read these stories to me growing up.

The Struwelpeter taught kids clear morals to specific

disastrous consequences of bad behavior.

A picture of our living room with our black & white TV.

Social gatherings with my family and friends.

Here, I'm "reading" a Russian magazine.

I always liked the pictures the most.

A snapshot of me in my great-grandmother's garden.

My brother and me lounging in front of my dad's beehives.

Our first day of school.

You can see me with my friend Rene'.

We are proudly holding our cones

filled with goodies & some school

supplies.

Exiting the school after a tour of the classroom.

(First Grade)

The Trabant. We waited "forever" to get one of these.

Today, they are considered a "cult-classic."

Glossary:

Ampelmann: The Ampelmännchen is a beloved
symbol in Eastern Germany "enjoy[ing] the
privileged status of being one of the few
features of communist East Germany to have
survived the end of the Iron Curtain with his
popularity unscathed." After the fall of the Berlin
Wall, the Ampelmännchen acquired cult status
and became a popular souvenir item in the
tourism business.

Berlin Wall: was a barrier that
divided Berlin from 1961 to 1989. Constructed
by the German Democratic Republic (GDR, East
Germany), starting on 13 August 1961, the Wall
completely cut off (by land) West Berlin from
surrounding East Germany and from East
Berlin until government officials opened it in
November 1989. Its demolition officially began
on 13 June 1990 and was completed in
1992. The barrier included guard towers placed
along large concrete walls, which circumscribed
a wide area (later known as the "death strip")
that contained anti-vehicle trenches, "fakir

beds" and other defenses. The **Eastern Bloc** claimed that the Wall was erected to protect its population from fascist elements conspiring to prevent the "will of the people" in building a **socialist state** in East Germany. In practice, the Wall served to prevent the massive **emigration and defection** that had marked East Germany and the communist Eastern Bloc during the post-World War II period.

Currywurst: is often sold as a **take-out/take-away food**, Schnellimbisse (snacks), at **diners** or "greasy spoons," on children's menus in **restaurants**, or as a **street food**. Usually served with **french fries** or **bread rolls** (Brötchen), it is popular all over Germany but particularly popular in the metropolitan areas of Berlin, **Hamburg**, and the **Ruhr Area**. Considerable variation both in the type of sausage used and the ingredients of the sauce occurs between these areas.

DDR: East Germany, formally the **German Democratic Republic** or **GDR** (German: *Deutsche Demokratische Republik* (**DDR**), was a state in the **Eastern Bloc** during the **Cold War** period.

From 1949 to 1990, it administered the region of Germany that was occupied by Soviet forces at the end of World War II—the Soviet Occupation Zone of the Potsdam Agreement, bounded on the east by the Oder–Neisse line. The Soviet zone surrounded West Berlin, but did not include it; as a result, West Berlin remained outside the jurisdiction of the GDR. The German Democratic Republic was established in the Soviet Zone, while the Federal Republic was established in the three western zones.

Pionier Organization: The Ernst Thälmann Pioneer Organisation, consisting of the **Young Pioneers** and the **Thälmann Pioneers**, was a youth organization of schoolchildren aged 6 to 14, in East Germany. They were named after Ernst Thälmann, the former leader of the Communist Party of Germany who was executed at the Buchenwald concentration camp.

The group was a subdivision of the *Freie Deutsche Jugend* (FDJ, Free German Youth, East Germany's youth movement. It was founded on 13 December 1948 and broke apart in 1989 on German reunification. From the 1960s and 1970s, nearly all schoolchildren between ages 6 and 14 were organized into Young Pioneer or Thälmann Pioneer groups.

The pioneer group was based on the Scouts but organized in such a way as to teach schoolchildren aged 6 – 14 socialist ideology and prepare them for the *Freie Deutsche Jugend*, the FDJ. Its organization was similar to scouting and other such organizations. Afternoons spent at the pioneer group mainly consisted of a mixture of adventure, myth-like socialist teaching and the upkeep of revolutionary traditions. In the summer, children usually went to pioneer camps similar to the **West German** *Wandervogel* groups or the **Scouts**. International pioneer camps were also common, intended to foster friendship between different nationalities.

Trabant is a car that was produced by former **East German** auto maker **VEB Sachsenring Automobilwerke Zwickau** in **Zwickau, Saxony**. It was the most common vehicle in **East Germany** and was also exported to countries both inside and outside the **Eastern Bloc**.

Due to its outdated and inefficient **two-stroke engine** (which produced poor fuel economy for its low power output and thick, smoky exhaust), and production shortages, the Trabant was regarded with derisive affection as a symbol of the extinct former East Germany and of the fall of the **Eastern Bloc.**

Konsum: a state-controlled retailer in the former **German Democratic Republic**

Kindergarten: East Germany accomplished a large-scale education reform and introduced a dense network of high-standard education facilities, especially **kindergartens**. A unique characteristic of East German kindergartens was the strong educational background of these institutions, even compared to today's kindergartens in Germany. Children from age three to six learned to interact with other children got used to a stable daily routine and were introduced to the idea of **learning**. There was no teaching of reading, writing or arithmetic, but the fundamental concepts were taught to develop intellectual and motor skills. For instance, introduction to set theory within the numbers up to 10, counting up to 20, handling of quantities, crafts and motor skills exercises to prepare the handwriting, the handling of pencils, scissors, fabrics and glue, and other skills.

Children were also encouraged to take an active role in the running of their kindergartens. Children often served each other meals and helped keep the kindergarten clean and tidy.

Information in the glossary was obtained/ gathered from - Source: Wikipedia.com

About the Author:

Antje grew up in East Germany and always had a sense of adventure. After the fall of the German Wall in 1989, she could not wait to leave her home and see other places in the world to meet new people and gather different perspectives.

Now, she is a wife and mom of two teenagers living in eastern Pennsylvania. As her kids grew up, she realized how important it is to tell her childhood story to them. Not only, because the world she grew up in no longer exists, but also to correct any false impressions they might receive from other people.

While writing this book for her children, and talking about her background with coworkers and friends who were captivated by it, she was determined to share her story with others as well.

Contact:

Antje.Arnold@writeme.com

https://www.amazon.com/Antje-Arnold/e/B07H9C3P4L

Her book received an honorable mention at 2018 The Hollywood Book Festival.

Dankeschön!!

Printed in Great Britain
by Amazon